NOBODY BELIEVES CRAZY

By

WILL MORRO

ISBN-13: 9798649380317
KINDLE ASIN: B08B5K7PFX

An Imprint of Stay Thirsty Publishing

A Division of

STAY THIRSTY MEDIA, INC.
A News and Entertainment Company
staythirsty.com

WILL MORRO

NOBODY BELIEVES CRAZY

Chapter 1
The Label of My New Mental Illness

The negative stigma that tends to go with mental disorders can be felt through silence alone. Not everybody relates to what you are going through. It's something that you constantly struggle with on a day-to-day basis and is a topic that just doesn't come up in typical conversations. I was with a family member and brought up something about being bipolar and an experience I had in the psych ward. I tend to lack a filter with some of my stories and often say a little too much. However, after bringing up my condition in a casual conversation, my family member told me later that I really shouldn't tell people those kinds of things. I got the sense that he felt it was not something I should bring up because it can be off-putting. People, even family members, just don't understand that it's just part of your life. People in general can be taken aback by the discussion of mental disorders; it's just not a kind of topic that people feel comfortable talking about because they simply are not familiar with the right way to approach that kind of thing. Early on, struggling to figure out the disorder in your own mind, you find out it's that much more challenging as much of what you are grappling with is personal and you are stuck going it alone. Sure, there are other people that can relate, but so much of what you're dealing with is unique to your own psychosis, even with doctors and therapists, much of the burden for stability, piece of mind, and personal answers rest on you and you alone.

Bipolar disorder carries an incredible negative stigma. Kanye West put out an album where he claimed on one of his tracks: "It's not a disability; it's a superpower." I don't expect the average Joe to understand that one bit. I understand it in its entirety. It's not just some rush or a quick wave of some heightened state or emotion. It's a state of being -- mania -- that completely takes over. Empowered. Sure. Untouchable and invincible. Likely. Enlightened and free. Why not? Sheer ecstasy, even under false cognition.

Personally, I don't have too much of a problem with bipolar being classified as a disorder or a disability. If you have to take time off work because of what's going on in your own head, then the label is justifiable. What irks me is the idea that bipolar disorder, as it is often defined, is a *mood* disorder. I hate this definition because the word mood is only used in a negative light not to mention that it is followed by the word disorder. There are way more people in our society that are moody and have mood disorders than there are people with bipolar disorder. I cannot stand people who self-diagnose themselves with bipolar disorder because people often call them moody so that becomes their excuse. When the word mood is used to define bipolar disorder, it is used to explain mania -- a heightened state of existence -- and depression - a state of existence of complete loss. A moody person believing they have a mood disorder such as bipolar is probably a very emotional person, but personally, I feel like this notion that moody people are, in fact, bipolar misrepresents the disorder itself.

How does one come to terms with a diagnosis of bipolar disorder?

I can only attack this question with my own personal account after being diagnosed with Bipolar I Disorder at the age of twenty.

First week of my second semester sophomore year of college; drop/add week. All my core requirements to graduate college with any degree were complete. Entering college with an undecided major and after three semesters, not much had changed. It was time to pick the classes that were to decipher the rest of my time in college and life thereafter. I was still undecided and was at a loss trying to figure out what kind of major was right for me. Worse yet, school was the furthest thing on my mind. Was there a girl in mind? There's always a girl in mind and that only added to my own dilemma and personal strife. Six days into drop/add week and I hadn't gone to a single class. Sleep quickly became an afterthought as my world was unraveling and turning upside down. Food was not necessary. I was running on steam and became fixated on figuring out this imaginary puzzle that I created that would somehow solve all my problems. I was feeling invigorated; at the top of the world, but thankfully my college roommate took notice of my erratic behavior. Right before things really went awry, he made the call to my mom and told her I had lost it. My mom flew out to Boston right as I attempted to publicly propose to a girl who had dumped me months ago. I was head over heels bonkers thinking that this manic episode was the feeling of love; far from the truth.

After being pulled out of college and evaluated in a hospital's psychiatric department, I awoke many hours later to find myself walled-in and in quite a different environment than ever thought imaginable. Such an abstract setting that even after my three-week stay I had not begun to accept the place I was admitted to. Mental Institution. Doesn't make any sense. Not me. *No big deal*, I thought to myself. You get out and think, *I'm out now and everything is back to normal. Just a little speed bump.* Yeah right! More like a life changing cliff of which I was now faced with trying to climb for the rest of my life.

Put on a med regime, regular doctor visits, and now grappling with my new label; a label known for having a negative stigma: mental disorder. Nobody, and I'd bet my bottom dollar on it, I mean nobody, can just snap back to reality, the real world, without an immense amount of time; time to think, reflect, learn, relearn, analyze, and figure out what this disorder means to that person and that person alone -- forget having to grapple with others' perceptions, questions, and misguided and misdirected judgments; these people are just the background noise to the problem you yourself have to tackle. Coming to grips with your own scrambled thought process, your illogical actions, and the imaginary reality you created is one of the hardest tasks you will ever face in your life. Can you do it in weeks? How about months? It took me about five years. And even after those five years it took about nine years for me to really feel comfortable and ready to engage others openly about how my bipolar works and how it happens to affect me.

What did they do in the mental institution that could leave someone in a mental quandary for up to five years?

When I underwent my first manic episode, I became hyper-aware. I was paying attention to every detail put in front of me.

Data of what was going on around me was being picked up, stored, processed, categorized, and analyzed to the extreme. I was trying to find reason with just about everything that was happening in my life. It quickly surmounted to the point where my mind was on overdrive and running loose. It's as if as though any and all things could possibly mean something, and I was making it all fit together as if there were some deeper meaning or meaning at all. My mind was running on overload, couldn't stop, and digesting so much information that it was churning out complete nonsense. It spiraled out of control quickly like a deck of cards being splattered across the room; alone in my room in deep thought for a solid five days with little human reaction, and suddenly I took action on what I believed was going on. I went about on a campus-wide search to marry the girl I had become fixated on. The reality was that I was scaring everybody, and it was time for intervention. My mom, uncle, and roommate coaxed me into a car, and they sped off to Newton Wellesley Hospital, where I'd spend my next three weeks.

After being admitted to the hospital, I spent time reflecting on my own mental state. Something that most people don't do enough of. I attempted to explain myself to one nurse in particular and thought that the answer I was fixated on finding was still out there. After hearing myself fail to make any logical connections when explaining what I thought was going on in my life, I found myself in a new and terrible disposition. I was not making any sense. There was just too much scrambled data, and it was hard listening to myself talk in circles without ever being able to have a truly logical connection about the past few weeks of my life and, furthermore, there was just no way to justify the ridiculous things I was saying and worse yet doing.

Even my behavior in the psych ward showed clear signs of trouble. Not only was I trying to talk my way out of the hospital's diagnosis, I was plotting my escape; this is something I still do to this day when admitted to psych wards. It's like the line from *Shawshank Redemption* states, "Get busy living or get busy dying." I had it all figured out. Somehow I had collected just enough money from other patients in the unit to pay for my train fare. I was so proud of myself as I truly believed that was the test that I was up against the entire time. I went right to the nurse that I had begun opening up to and showed her the money I collected and expected her to open the doors for me so that I could see my way out and go back to my life in college. Clearly the weight of what was happening had not yet begun to sink in.

The psych ward visit was completely justified, and they took the necessary measures to break me down; and boy did I break. A year and a half into college, having completed all of my core requirements, taking top-end math classes, and holding onto a GPA near 3.5, my whole life took an unreal turn. White walls, no windows, a homeless roommate or two, and nothing to do except walk around the square hospital floor trying to figure out how to get out. Reality to me was still not in tune with public perception. The first day I was released, I had a friend who said jokingly, "Good to have you back from the clink." Even after being in the place for three whole weeks, I wasn't ready to hear something like that. In my mind I still hadn't even really come to grips with this notion that I was in a mental hospital. Furthermore, the hospital visit had taken its toll on me and I couldn't just shrug off the comment or turn it into a laughing matter.

Chapter 2
Adjusting to Shock

It is impossible to just let go of the feelings and life you create in a manic episode. The feelings are too real even if everybody around you is trying to get you to see past the mirage you have created for yourself. Like I said -- they broke me down mentally. Around the three-week mark, I got on the hospital's payphone and cracked. I called my mom and just cried. I couldn't live in this place any longer, I couldn't address living in my own mind not knowing how to explain myself when I knew there was no way ... I admitted defeat. My reality was off-kilter and I was willing/had to accept it. Anything to get me out of this place. Living in a room on a regimented schedule, lining up for food without having to look at the time, no windows or natural light, no way to expel any stored-up energy, changing roommates because the homeless person you're sharing a room with decides to piss all over the floor, total misunderstanding on how you ended up in this place to begin with. I broke down and was granted release. The catch? The catch was that even though this hospital completely broke me down, once I was released the next phase took place; figuring out what in the world just happened to me; putting things back together, if possible, and trying to figure out a new sense of who you truly are and gaining self-confidence in a circumstance that leaves the task nearly impossible. It's not just the rug getting swept away under your feet, it's like the whole floor collapsing. The endeavor to find solace and peace of mind in order to take control of this mental disorder is now part of your endless ongoing journey.

The medicine and drugs they give you suck. They're not fun drugs where you get a sweet buzz or high. Personally, my drug experience has been a huge challenge. The drugs the doctors prescribe me tend to affect me subtly on a mental level and it's extremely hard to find the right med regime, as many of the meds take time to really play a factor in your life. Not to mention, my regular regime of drinking and smoking pot made it even more challenging to find meds that really could fit. There is no cure to date; in the end, it's practicing medicine. The only way to get the right mix is to be open to trying things out and working toward something that keeps you level; discover it, challenge it, question it, but do your part to help figure it out. I've heard story after story about people with bipolar disorder not taking their meds because of the terrible side effects. Not me. If society deems that a med regime is what I need to be a functioning part, then I accept.

The immediate impact these meds had on my life were obvious. I took a semester of college off and re-enrolled the following fall. Within six months I gained 70 pounds. Imagine walking into a school 70 pounds heavier than the last time you saw all your friends, not to mention you are recently diagnosed with a mental disorder. Socially, both the weight gain and the recent diagnosis were big hurdles, but worse, school became an utter challenge. Reading anything became an almost impossible task. Perhaps the best way to explain it is that after my original manic episode my mind was just focused on so many things it became hard to concentrate on one or two things. Classes went from being an afterthought to becoming practically unbearable. Sleeping was a whole nother challenge. With all the meds I was taking and the extra weight I had put on, suddenly I was sleeping almost 15 hours a day. These past few things were just the obvious changes I was dealing with, and things that I had no choice but to confront head on.

Mental stability -- this was the real challenge I faced for the remaining years I was in college and something that I know I will always be dealing with the rest of my life. First off, you don't just accept this notion that you are a crazy person. Forget that. I'm a fighter and I sure as hell was willing to fight that idea right where it stands. Honestly, it probably took me three years to finally stop the fight. I eventually came to the conclusion that bipolar is just the case they gave me, and I needed to stop trying to battle against the idea that I had a mental disorder and instead own it.

Chapter 3
Not Ready for Life

It got pretty eerie in my later years in college. All my friends and their friends knew about my current mental condition. With all my classmates it often felt like there was a giant elephant in the room that nobody was attempting to address. It was by no means a fault of theirs whatsoever. If anyone was going to address the elephant, it had to be me. It was better left untouched. I still hadn't figured this diagnosis out and wasn't ready to talk about it. I couldn't explain it to my friends because at the time I still couldn't explain it to myself; the elephant had to remain in place. Moreover, I needed the elephant to block tackling an issue where I had no answer to or any way of explaining to the kids at school where my head was at. Getting high and forgetting the problems I was facing was the easy way out. However, it became a challenge to grow with my classmates and engage anyone on a personal level as I seemingly had lost touch with who I was. College life moves fast. In one class onto the next and then hit the parties for the never-ending social scene. I could no longer keep up with any of it; something that I never had trouble with beforehand.

How can one take control over their disorder and stop manic or depressive episodes?

I met with my doctor for the first time after being originally diagnosed. My first question; Will this happen again? "Yes, undoubtedly," my doctor simply put it with confidence. In my head I'm thinking: Are you serious? I have to go through this shit repeatedly for the rest of my life. No warning and suddenly your entire life gets shredded apart all over again. This doesn't seem like fun. The only answer to date; take your meds and get sleep; preventative medicine at its finest. As you grow back into yourself over time your mind gets stronger. You begin to learn the difference between rational thoughts and irrational thoughts. Compartmentalizing your own logic and creating a system of checks and balances where you constantly question your own actions. The idea being able to prove to yourself and others, if necessary, that your actions are well thought out, rational, and justifiable. Keeping track of your train of thought and double-checking, even if it's a day later or after a good night's sleep, is important to show that what you are doing is logical. It may seem silly, but often I find myself thinking of these great ideas and things I want to go about doing. I tell myself to keep it in mind and decide whether or not it's a good idea after a solid night's sleep. Even in one action-packed day your mind can quickly begin to ramp up. The thing about this ramping up notion is that it's quite a rush; it's awesome. Suddenly you forget to sleep, eating becomes an afterthought, and quickly you can find yourself up for days. Being stable and on your medication doesn't guarantee that you are not capable of acting impulsively. Keeping yourself in constant check becomes a vital part of the self-monitoring needed to protect yourself from ending up back in a mental institution.

College ended. I passed, barely. No job offers, that's for sure. Living at home with mom and dad with no future plans. Things were looking bleak. Still had no grasp on the bipolar diagnosis. Still a shell of myself. It's as if I had become an introvert just so I never had to confront what I had morphed into. Watching television in my parents' basement and my mom came down and said, "Will, what do you love more than anything in the world?" The answer was simple: Golf. "Get your resume together, we're driving you all over Chicago and you're applying to courses." I ended up scoring a job at a public course in Winnetka as a cart cleaner and range operator. I held the seasonal job for the next two seasons. It offered hope. Perhaps, despite all my problems, I could work in the golf industry starting from the bottom. It didn't help that I had no unique skills when playing a full round, but I was filled with the notion that I could eventually become a golf pro.

The 2011 season ended, and I was about to face another Chicago winter. Winters were tough on me as I often found myself jobless and having to leech off the support of my parents to get by.

Chapter 4
My Take on Depression

How can depression affect your life?

Depression is a tough one for me. Hopelessness is a big part of depression. It can envelope every bit of your existence. I tend to deny the notion that depression has any affect on my life. I like to think that I have an attitude that blocks the feeling state that most people describe as a depressive state. Reflecting on my own circumstances in life I find myself feeling down and out and even moved to tears. "Keep fighting," I tell myself time and time again. "Wipe off the tears and find a way out." Get restless with any type of complacency and dig yourself out of the rut. Faith plays a large part in my life. Having the inner belief that life is good, that humanity is good, that things happen for a reason, and that hope really does spring eternal. The "ruts" I find myself in can be overwhelming and truly affect my mood a great deal; mopey, sad, anxious, irritated, and mad. Having to start over in life, start from the beginning, as I have so often, can truly bring out these emotions and I know I can characterize myself as being depressed. NO COMPLACENCY. I fight these feelings as soon as I recognize them. If I didn't … depression can begin to win, to take over, and only make matters worse. I am lucky. I have had the support of my family throughout my life. They have been motivators on many occasions when depression has the chance to win and take over. I am also lucky to be extremely self aware of the warning signs of my depression as I have the attitude and the fight within me to pick myself up and get through each day, each hour, and deeply believe that if I can just carry on life will lead me down a more promising path.

My life post-college had become stagnant. I held a seasonal job for minimum wage and winters only brought out the feeling of hopelessness. I had trouble finding a winter job as I made the mistake of only looking for seasonal employment in the 2010-

2011 winter season. My passion for golf was the only thing driving my motivation to work. My second winter out of college came on quick, and it appeared that I was in for more drudgery. Something needed to happen. I needed a change. I needed warm weather. I needed work to feel self-worth. At the end of September my mom was flying down to Hawaii to help my aunt and uncle move. The two of them happened to live down there and also happened to be big time golfers. This was it. I told my mom to buy me a one-way ticket to Hawaii as I planned to leave Chicago and try my luck on the Big Island. The stipulation; I had two weeks to find a job and lodging upon arrival, and if I managed to do that I wouldn't have to fly back home.

Chapter 5
Refuge in a Fresh Start

Three days. Three days in my new surrounding and driving around the island in a rental car from the airport, I had a job and a month-month rental apartment. It appeared that I had an opportunity for a fresh start and a new beginning as an inhabitant on the island of Hawaii. Things were looking my way, and this yielded all kinds of hope. Not only could I take a larger amount of accountability for my life and take care of myself, but I was free from areas in my life where my illness was known to others and weighed heavily on my mind as I had clear trouble coping with the negative stigma that I perceived had relevancy.

Hawaii changed it all.

My life was monitored. Drinking, smoking, everything, my parents watched it all. I was carefully watched. Living in Hawaii I became free. Suddenly the drinking I did was no longer frowned upon or recorded. I could be myself. I COULD BE MYSELF. For the first time in many years -- since I've been living with the diagnosis of bipolar disorder -- I could pretend that shit never even existed. Before going to Hawaii, I had been lying to my parents. I was drinking alcohol; and not by great lengths, but periodically and not in great amounts. My aunt and uncle, who lived on the island where I was starting my new beginning, were extraordinarily supportive. They understood that I had and was accountable for my own personal life. My mom or dad had never been so understanding.

My diagnosis of Bipolar I Disorder was never my own personal business or my own personal struggle. My parents had always played a large part in the diagnosis from the beginning, and they had always viewed the diagnosis not only as a disability but as a problem that they needed to account for. One day my mom came to a meeting with me and my psychiatrist and talked about how my life was a wash; as if my life was never going to amount to anything. I was appalled. I stood firm, I stood my ground, I explained to my mom in front of my doctor that I disagreed with her point blank. My life was not a wash at all. I refused to believe that my life was a failure. I screamed, "My life is not a failure." I truly believed that my life had hope, had meaning, had a purpose. My life, despite the belief of my parents, was not a failure. I knew deep down that being bipolar and the struggles that came with the illness were not a death sentence; there was always hope. I was shocked; my mom accepted that my life was, sadly, lost and unimportant. I stood firm and exclaimed in front of my doctor that I felt differently. Given all I had been through didn't matter. I had purpose. My life wasn't a waste. There was more to my life then appearances let on, and there was more to my life than my mom might have understood at the time. I had hope and belief that my life had reason to the rhyme even though it couldn't be understood. I never gave up on my own relevancy, and it was a shock that my mom and dad had given up. In their mind, I lost, I not only wasn't going to amount to anything, but I simply was incapable of living up to the potential that I originally could have been capable of. It did hurt; hearing this from my mom in front of my doctor of twelve years; knowing that my parents felt this way. My gut reaction -- I was pissed. I never, for one second, felt as if my life was a failure. I didn't see it that way. How dare my parents for seeing things that way. Fuck that! I got hope. I always got hope. I don't look at my life as a failure. Bad investment, sure ... no doubt about it ... but failure; no way, no how; I got too much fight in me to chalk my life up to a failure. I'll never stop fighting. No way I can look at myself as a charity case as I am simply not done fighting. It's hard. It's hard making people understand who you are. I'm still working on it. People don't understand that you have different priorities in life; they don't understand that you have different benchmarks that define success. The truth about mental illness is that there is a negative stigma attached to it; a negative stigma that outsiders, others, apply to the disorder. Unfortunately for me, my parents were not the exception to this notion. It's been an ongoing theme throughout my fight.

I escaped. Forget the fact that after working two weeks in my new job in Hawaii I got fired. It didn't shake me one bit. No doubt that after earning my new life on the big island, I had lost my job, but in a matter of half an hour, I picked up a new job at a completely different golf course. It was meant to be. My dream of living and moving to Hawaii was alive, and I needed the fresh start.

New set of friends, a job that fit my personality, a living situation that I loved, and a ton of free golf. I was twenty-five-years old and for the first time since being diagnosed with bipolar disorder I had nobody judging me for who I was and/or their preconceived notions of what was really going on in my head. I was free of any stigma or judgment with the people I met and became friends with. It made things a lot easier. Getting to be myself had become hard for me in the past five years. Moving to Hawaii I really had a shot at rediscovering the person I had left behind back in college. Unfortunately, I kind of turned my nine-month stay in Hawaii into extended college. Even though I lucked into a full time job working course maintenance at an amazing public course on the island, I had not only lost my work ethic and was not doing a good enough job of taking things at work seriously enough, but I was spending too much money at the local bars. I might have been in Hawaii, but I wasn't making it on my own and the dream was not sustainable.

Chapter 6
The Importance of Failing

My last three weeks on the island were as important as any three weeks of my entire life. It's funny the things you remember. My first few days on the island I got into a conversation with a gardener at my Aunt and Uncle's house. He said welcome to the island and all that stuff, but he also said something that I'll never forget; As if to call it all out, he said, "Remember Will, you can stay here as long as you want, but the island has a funny way of getting rid of you." As is with all advice I get I take this with a grain of salt, but I do not fully ignore it. People tell you things about what they know or what they think about you, and even if they're a downright nutso, I find that it's important to reflect on their perspective on things even if it's just for a little bit. You get told things for a reason, about yourself or about the world; it doesn't hurt to at least pretend to take it seriously. Anyway, life was really changing on the island and I was failing to respond. My Aunt and Uncle had left the island and about the same time my best friend had also departed. I was letting it blow up in my face. Maybe it was because I didn't have someone to talk to and right the ship, but it was getting scary for me; I was losing important friends. I panicked. I decided I needed to look for new work. I was only three weeks away from my final review at my current job. If I passed this review, I would have been part of the Union and earned a job and my own place at work. Things at work were a little shaky. I wasn't the model employee, but things were starting to click. I was getting into work shape and taking on a lot of the tougher roles. It took six months and a lot of doubt from my boss as well as my coworkers, but I was getting there. If I didn't start freaking out about the future job review, if I just kept my head down, I would've been just fine.

"The island has a funny way of getting rid of you." I was on a mission of self-sabotage; for no reason. Last three weeks on the island. I started to do a lot of self-reflection. I had become a better person and had a stronger sense of myself than ever before. I began writing my life's philosophy in length on my computer. I was dissecting my own mind, but I was also picking myself apart. Suddenly things started to have meaning. I was no longer living in the present. I was trying to pick up on clues. Sure enough, I left my job at the golf course a week before my union review. I left it for a job I found on Craigslist. A sure thing, or everything but. The job was to film tourists at a junky snorkel location and try to sell the tape. It was a complete joke. I wasn't thinking clearly. Not only that; after my second day the guy giving me the job told me he wasn't going to hire me. My time on the island was already getting itchy. I made sure it was absolutely over.

Those last few weeks on the island I slipped into mania. I probably spent two weeks in more of a hypomanic state. In these two weeks I wrote ten pages about who and where I was in life; a document that is true to my nature so much that even though I was on the verge of insanity when I wrote it, it feels very real. The paper examined my argument to get into heaven. As deep as that sounds, it is a paper, not about right and wrong, but about what I feel matters most in my life. It answers what I am looking for and examines a sort of funny philosophy: this notion that I have a right to be in heaven because of the rules, arbitrary as they may be, that I put together based on sports; the sports I loved most and the rules that these sports teach us; as if the sports themselves give me a guideline for my sexual exploits. It's completely made up, but it feels right. It's a philosophy that I adhere to this day. Not because I think it to be true, but it just feels right. Even though I came up with it during a time I was considerably unstable, or at least reaching that state, doesn't take away the meaning this philosophy I put together means to me.

Taken out of college in the middle of my sophomore year, I met with a psychiatrist. I told him that I was going to write a paper for him the next time we met. The paper was my life philosophy at the time. I wanted to show the doctor exactly who he was dealing with. I wrote one page. I don't remember everything I wrote, but the first line was, "Life is an argument." In my mind, arguing your own existence mattered. What was my argument? I figured it out in Hawaii. It all came down to what I loved most: sports. Hockey, football, baseball -- in that order; best for last.

In my waning days at the golf course I also came to the realization, even though my two weeks were in, that I knew in my heart of hearts I was a good worker. I knew that whatever job I had moving forward, I was going to be able to tackle the challenge of that job the right way. The course maintenance job I got in Hawaii was my first full-time job since waiting tables in college. Going into the job I had lost what it takes to be a value in the workplace; confidence in myself and knowing myself was a large part of that. It's hard to be a part of a team at work if you are unsure of who you are and your own capabilities; coupled with not being able to express yourself properly, and even with a college degree, I had to learn what it takes to work again and how I managed myself in the workplace. I mean, look, at the first job I had on the Big Island, I worked at a golf course in the pro shop and ran the register. Sadly enough, I couldn't handle money. People would pay me cash for their rounds of golf, and I would start shaking uncontrollably. No wonder I got fired. Sometimes easy little things that we take for granted in life become triggers for your own emotions, and therefore, become excessively challenging.

Leaving the island was challenging. I skipped out on my first flight home to Chicago because I thought I was going to make the plane crash. My mind was on overload. I was connecting dots that were on separate pages. Thanks to one of my closest friends on the island, I eventually got on board a flight home. Life was eternally different in my mind; I had a vision for how to live the rest of my life and I meant to see that vision out.

Chapter 7
Ready to Work and Live

Life back in the city, back in my parents' basement, hit me pretty hard. The winter of 2012 was not one to remember. I was at square zero all over again. I had no job and no prospects, and I was coming off a pretty crazy manic episode experienced back in Hawaii. I swung into depression. Laying face-up on my bed, eyes open, motionless, for days on end. I had no reason to push forward. I lacked hope. I had no reason to live, nonetheless, get myself out of bed. As is the case, time pushed forward and the seasons changed. Eventually, we ran into the spring of 2013. The weather improved and so did my outlook on life. I acquired a skill working at golf courses in Hawaii, and it was time for me to prove it.

Turned in my application at the local public course in the city. Got a job immediately. There was still life left in me yet. The job I could do, but I was only killing time. It was a seasonal gig and didn't pay much. I was 26 and still living with my folks. I wasn't happy, and the season was coming to an end. What's next? Another winter laying in bed. I had no exit strategy.

So I'm chewing on an apple in my parents garden. Neighbor lady approaches, we've exchanged pleasantries here and there. I'm in a good mood. She asks, "Hey Will, do you like sports?" "Ya," I continued chewing. With the season just about over, my wonderful neighbor tells me to send my resume to her husband, who is starting a sports company. Just my luck. Thanks apple.

Timing couldn't have been better. A new start-up, winter work, and the possibility of a career. I spent a total of seven minutes interviewing with two different high-ups in the company and lucked my way into a job. I was ready. The mania was under control. The depression was far past. My old self that I found in Hawaii was shining. I was over a year sober and ready to take on anything put in front of me. Not only that, the job was in sports. How could I fail? Sports were my life. I literally had a philosophy on life geared toward the subject. The rest is anything but history.

Chapter 8
Understanding My Own Illness

I hate writing. It is a nuisance and a chore. When do I write? I write when I need to get things on paper. Do I need to organize my thoughts? Does my line of reasoning need to be proven someplace other than my own head? Am I putting things down trying to dig for more? Am I in search of deeper meaning? Does part of my life need to be documented because it's just too unbelievable? YES! Do you have any idea how hard it is for me to write just one paragraph? I sit at my computer and dribble out a relevant point or something catchy and my mind jumps around from story to story -- experience to experience -- and I have to focus just to keep my own train of thought so that I can be poignant or some shit. I don't try to write very often. I write because I have to. I have to get my story across, or express my point of view, or because I am lost and there's no other answer.

People with mental illnesses, specifically what I have; Bipolar I Disorder; we tend to create emotions from things that simply aren't true. It can be pretty damn hard snapping back to reality. The big problem I have is how real everything in my life seems to be and I'm left denying and suppressing, not just emotions, but actual events that I know deep down, despite being unbelievable, actually took place. My first time in the psych ward I had to face these crazy emotions and feelings; come to learn that they were quite a bit off-kilter. But having to deny things that really do happen to me, that's why I'm writing now. How do I deny events in my life because things that happen to me just don't happen to people? Should I be denying my own reality just because if you tell people about what's really happening in your life, they might stick you back in the mental institution? I guess it just means that it's time to start writing. At least the paper you're writing on won't roll its eyes at you and decide that you're full of shit; the kick -- you're already medically and legally crazy. The stories you tell, no matter how much truth, have no ground to stand on; your stories can't be true. You're like the guy who saw aliens and you keep going around telling everybody that aliens exist. It's too unbelievable, but it sure as hell all happened. The problem is simple; nobody believes crazy.

When did it all start? Octoberish 2018. I got off my meds starting mid-September of that year. Was I insane … hell no! I was holding my own; clear and clairvoyant. But boy-oh-boy the stars were feeling pretty damn in line, and there wasn't a thing in the world I wasn't ready for.

Chapter 9
Looking for Signs

Around the end of November 2014, I financed my first car. It's funny how some addictions start. I hate driving. But for some reason I couldn't get out of the driver's seat. I was working 5 days a week 9-hour shifts and I would spend over 4 hours every night driving around Chicago, listening to the radio, and watching the city lights (as I know, they were watching me). The addiction got worse and worse. I couldn't get away. I developed a pattern. Southbound to Roosevelt hang a right. Columbus to Balbo, another right. Swing a left back onto Lake Shore Drive going Northbound. All the way to the Bryn Mawr exit … flip back around onto the entrance ramp and start it all again. Doing nothing and harming nobody. Over and over. Again and again. I escaped to my car and used driving as a sanctuary and it definitely turned into therapy.

What do you mean the lights were watching you? Can't really explain it, just know that my radio became in-sync with certain patterns on the building lights. I knew pretty early on all that driving around had won me attention. One car night after night out doing loops on Lake Shore Drive for hours on end. Somebody took notice; of who or what I will never know. Pretty strange escape for a guy that hates driving. But there was more to it. Using all six of my radio presets, I would change the stations and depending on the stations I picked, so too would the colors of the lights on all the buildings change. BULLSHIT! I know. It's impossible to prove. There's a building as you head southbound and come to that first stoplight on the downtown stretch of Lake Shore Drive. The building has a big blue light strip across the top. Early on, this light strip changed all kinds of colors and would move to the beat of the song I was listening to on the radio. It would take on different colors depending on the mood of the song I was playing. It was so on point that it drove me mad. I took time off work because of mental instability in large part because I couldn't explain this light. I would work my way around the curve of the drive and I could guess the color of the light based solely on the song I was playing on my own car radio.

But you're right, it is bullshit or at least it had to be … that's what I kept telling myself. I decided that whoever is in charge of all the building lights must be listening to the exact same shit I'm listening to because the phenomenon was hard to ignore. Already marked with a pretty weird driving addiction, I figured it was best to keep this all to myself. The building lights were just the first major clue. I had the firm belief that even though I was alone in my car, eyes were on me. Nobody believes crazy. Something to note, but even more important, to ignore.

Was I lost? From every angle. My job was turning into a bust. I had no clue as to the career I was really meant for. I was driving around the city of Chicago in search of a sign. Just like I felt the first time I fell in love except this time around was slower. The process was longer. The reasons made sense and were justifiable. I just didn't know the right next move. So I drove looking for answers or clues. I was getting them in spades; hearts too. At one point the diamond building had a message in the middle. It simply said, "Marry her," right in the middle. Now if the lights of the city were keeping an eye on me, there couldn't have been a more direct message than that. The signs became addictive. I didn't see these things and go about trying to prove them to be true. I'm not stupid. I told myself, "It's all in your head." I was seeing a psychopharmacologist, but I never told him shit. He didn't even know that I had a pretty damn big crush, forget the notion that the city of Chicago is seemingly sending me messages. Nobody believes crazy; even I didn't believe this shit was happening. Way to coincidental and on a pretty massive scale. If what I was saying holds a bit of truth, I was being monitored at a pretty high level.

Yeah, I had this driving ordeal that was long from gone, but I knew deep down the girl of my dreams was in my life, and that's all I ever needed to know. I had been searching so hard for love in my life that I had simply given up, and even when she popped up out of nowhere, I was five ways to sideways too damn stubborn to make any of the right calls. Instead, I drove. Collected my thoughts, organized my feelings, arranged the proper tactical response, ignoring the silly city lights. Handle my shit despite all the shit that I must have been imagining.

Chapter 10
Learning to Express Pent Up Feelings

I had to make a move. When a man makes his mind up, he acts; otherwise he's not much of a man. Enough of the endless loops on Lake Shore Drive. Enough of the signs from every building light that lit up the Chicago skyline. The pitter patter had to come to an end. I needed to take actions and find answers. Woke up one morning and went out with co-workers to the local public course to play a round of golf before clocking in at work. Played the nine-hole golf course to perfection. Birdied the first three holes and forgot that the rest of the round even needed to be played. Just got thrown into one of those crazy moods. Felt like I had just played a perfect round of golf … decided it was the best round of my life. No better time to go all in. Showed up to the charade work had become. Said one sentence to all my co-workers and walked out. No questions asked. Not sure if I had just quit, but I definitely made a scene. I was trying to drive home some sort of coded point, and admittedly wasn't making much sense. Mania will do this to you. You start believing everyone is on the same page or wavelength as you are. The reality is that you're tampering with the deep end of psychosis and not making too much sense.

Got in my car after walking out of work and headed the long way home. As if the higher powers that be sent a message down to say, "Will, you're on overdrive … slow your role." I drive through a downtown city intersection. Sure enough, a cab driver flies through a red light and I pile straight into him. My phone, dead. No pen, plenty of witnesses. People in the crosswalk next to me were thanking me as there is a decent chance I saved lives hitting the cab driver. The problem here is that I was in la-la land. I was not prepared to handle this accident properly. I was handed two business cards from witnesses to the accident, but I promptly threw them out. For some reason I decided that the accident didn't need to be reported; everything will work out for the best, I thought to myself. Nobody got hurt and that was what was most important. The feelings in my life were taking control and I was losing control. My focus was on the girl at my office, and I was not making rational decisions as I thought things were all happening for a reason. I was manic and was making choices that, at the time, I thought were altruistic, but were, nevertheless, quite stupid.

Having just left work (debatable on whether or not I quit), getting into a huge car accident ($7,000 worth of damage to my car alone), I was still restless to show my feelings and make a move on a co-worker that I was head over heels for, and mixed with hypomanic or manic actions, I was determined to drive home my point of view. A point of view that I had to learn she just wasn't ready for. With a going away party for one of the members of our company that night, I prepared myself … honestly, for jack shit. I was acting like a fifth-grade idiot doing stupid lovey-dovey shit; it lacked any type of smoothness and was stretching the line of pathetic.

So I show up to this party later that night and park my car in the valet section. I pull my keys out of my car, walk up to the valet driver, and say, "That's the car." Apparently, this was convincing enough and there were no further questions. I was riding one hell of a high. In my mind nothing was going to stop me. I was setting up for something big and acting like a big shot.

Sometimes you can walk into a room and you pick up on a vibe right away. Got to the bar walking in like I was on the VIP list. I knew immediately that I had made a pretty big judgment error. I called my shot and completely missed. Here I was ready to pour my heart out for this girl from work, but she simply wasn't there yet. Shit wasn't gonna go my way and I wasn't sticking around trying to explain my antics that day. Figured I had some more thinking to do, didn't stick around the bar that night waiting for answers. I was in and out in less than two minutes. With my prime-time parking spot, I ditched my car and flagged down a cab.

Whenever a person gets a psychiatric evaluation, and I don't know if it's specific to Bipolar, but the first question the doctor will always ask you -- "Are you a harm to yourself or anybody else" -- if you answer is "no" to both, then essentially your considered okay and good to go. There is, and often, if not always, should be a few basic follow-up questions. I'm explaining this to you because it is important to understand how my mania can build. I do not struggle much with depression, but killing myself scares the shit out of me. People don't just kill themselves when they're depressed. Mania can make a person do shit that is sure as hell life-threatening. When I jumped into the first cab that pulled up to the bar that night, I was running with intense emotions. If that first cab took me right to a hospital, brought me into an emergency room setting, and went about conducting a psychiatric evaluation, I would've been admitted no questions asked.

Rejection is hard on anyone, and everyone handles it differently. I have one of the worst ways of handling rejection. Combine that with mania or hypomania, and it can be deadly. I have trouble accepting rejection just like anybody else, but my answer to the problem is to find or start trouble. When I was back in college and I was originally dumped for the first time, I got downright blackout drunk. Decided I needed to get my ass kicked. I know, it's crazy, but that's how I react. Felt the pain of the breakup so much that I sought out to feel physical pain; pain that wasn't so abstract. After feeling pretty damn rejected the past night out, I went out looking for answers. How could something I felt so strongly about not have worked out. What was wrong with me, the world, and what did I have to do to prove my self worth.

It couldn't be just me. All this shit going on in my life; these very real feelings. These plans I'm suddenly coming up with in the last 24 hours. There was something I was missing. I needed to think and reassess my read on the situation. "Just drive," I told the cab. I had been driving around and around Chicago for eight straight months ... sitting in a cab, getting the passenger's perspective, and taking a moment to cool down was much needed. I knew I was experiencing mania and I knew I had to be hesitant before making further actions (with myself and others). They ask if you're a harm to yourself or anyone else. I was a harm to myself that night, not others.

Chapter 11
Looking for Answers/Looking for a Greater Truth

Needless to say, the cabby didn't really like this stranger getting in his car and saying just drive. He was definitely frightened and frazzled. "I'll pay," I said, "However long you drive, I'll pay." He said it was his last ride before he was going home. I said, "Where u live" . . . "Oak Park" . . . "Perfect take me to Oak Park . . . I got people there too. I'll pay." You could tell he wasn't convinced about that idea. I said, fine take me home. Gave him the address of the building I grew up in . . . a building all the way north on Lake Shore Drive. We're halfway to the first destination. I said to the cabby, play your music. Whatever you like to listen to and blast it -- we were on Lake Shore Drive, my spot. He put on the radio and was jamming to 107.5. I started freestyling off the beat of the radio. No doubt I was scaring this cabby to no end. We got to my old building and I said, "Take me to Navy Pier." Honestly, in the back of my head I'm thinking if I went to Navy Pier, she might be there waiting for me … no worries I reasoned past that … a little too crazy. We get to Navy Pier and I pay the fare. After the first payment went through, the cabby realized that driving me around for the night could be pretty lucrative. I convinced the driver that I'd pay him $200 cash if he drove me around Lake Shore Drive for a few hours. He agreed so we headed for an ATM and gas at the Roosevelt pumps.

The Roosevelt pumps, aka the BP gas station just off the drive on Roosevelt, is essentially the spot, in my own mind, that marks the Northside from the South Side. I frequented the Roosevelt pumps quite a bit driving my loop. I usually tried to get gas at the Foster pumps, but smokes and cream soda made the Roosevelt pumps a worthwhile stop in my nightly roundabout commute. Heading into the Roosevelt pumps late at night is always a little bit of a nuisance. There tends to be a squad loitering at the entrance of the gas station that harasses many of the patrons, looking to get free handouts. Not your typical homeless guy or two; young black men intimidating people for a buck and a laugh. Forget them anyways.

I went past the crew and proceeded to try to pull money from the ATM. Somehow, trying to pull out the $200 cash to pay the cabby, my card mysteriously got denied. Started to head back to the cabby who was waiting by one of the pumps. Of course, the squad saw me go to the ATM and had to start heckling me for dough. They wanted money from me, and I showed them my empty-ass wallet. I didn't like their approach, especially because those guys had no business posing as beggars. About to get back in the cab, I noticed a penny on the pavement right in front of me. I was still ticked off at these guys harassing me. I decided to start shit, and I knew exactly what I was getting into. I picked up that penny and flicked it kind of aggressively, but definitely pugnaciously, toward the crew out front of the gas station ... I said nothing, but my action did not go unnoticed.

What happened next? Well, first off, they all saw me flick that penny aggressively toward them. One guy stepped in place to handle me as I disrespected the group quite blatantly. I played it clean and calm. I was way out numbered not only by the crew but all the bystanders. This was by no means home turf and not protected. Race was an obvious factor in the ensuing exchange. Truthfully, what I did wasn't illegal or even that bad, but I was looking for trouble and could have easily found too much had I not been careful with the ensuing exchange.

I went in immediate defense mode. First, the guy who chose to handle the problem (me) threw an empty plastic bottle in my direction. This was going to get violent, guaranteed. My goal - try not to get jumped by the whole crew. I became subservient. "Yes, Sirs," "No, Sirs," and "My apology, Sir," became the only dialogue coming out of my mouth. Feet together and arms spread across with zero movement. I showed that I was defenseless and had no intention to try to defend myself. The guy, a big guy, kind of disheveled looking, wearing a big white t-shirt, berated me and marched up and down the packed gas station getting angrier and angrier. It was a strange experience as all spectators seemed to have his side. I was fighting this battle alone.

Eventually, the gentleman cracked. He was barking at me and soon enough started calling me "nigger this" and "nigger that." My resolve to agree with everything he said and apologize profusely angered him further. He wanted me to slip-up. He wanted me to go on the offensive. All eyes were on us. With arms spread apart, I knew it was coming. He charged me from five feet away, pissed off that I was making him look a little stupid in front of the crowd. The guy took a full swing across my face. The whole crowd gawked over the result. I ate the haymaker like I got a pat on the cheek. If I went down with that punch, I bet the beating wouldn't have stopped. But when I didn't even flinch and took the blow with no problem, I won the crowd. Not only did I win the crowd, but I won over the posse out front. Two men grabbed the guy who hit me and pulled him away. A shorter gentleman put his arm around my shoulder, leaned toward my ear, and asked, "Why'd you flick the penny in their direction?" "I worked to pick it up," was my simple response, and it was good enough. I was free to leave. Now the BP gas station at Roosevelt has a no loitering policy and an armed security officer on duty at all times.

Back in the cab; no money from the ATM, and the cabby was officially done driving my crazy ass around. He drove a little north and a little west. Kicked me out next to one of those bars with a bunch of pinball machines and arcade games. No time for reflection. No time for peace. No clue of my next move. Take a quick left away from the bar and start heading down an unfamiliar street. Start looking for my next cab. Don't have to walk too far before hailing the next one down. I get in, "Take me anywhere, I'll pay." -- "Get out." I leave, not looking for trouble. I walk in the dead of night. Fenced-in park on my left, well-lit surroundings. Still in the middle of the city. Still had a chance with the next cab. Sure enough, one rolls through. I get in. My demeanor has shifted. I act defeated, helpless, weak. I started the night looking for some sort of answer to a personal problem. I had just been through a whole nother eye-opening experience. The punch in the face must have been what I needed most. I was done fighting. I still had the itch to get driven around the city by cab drivers. Three or four cab rides ensue. Some long, some short. Where to? Nowhere. Some cabbies kicked me right out, others took me for a little ride. Where was I going or even trying to do? The answer was simple from the start … I wanted to find her and tell her how I felt.

Chapter 12
Signs Seemed Apparent/Things Felt Meant to Be

It's a funny thing about mania. Certain things happen that catch your attention. The incidence or incidences draw questions. More importantly, they tend to make you continually look for these types of incidences on a regular basis if not continuously. As mania takes a turn for the worse you begin to interweave and interconnect many things that probably have no place being bundled together. Usually, a deeper meaning for what is going on around you starts to develop. For instance, in one of my last cab rides I'm convinced to this day that I negotiated the standard price for regular gas at $3.00. You can say what you want, but since that negotiation with a cab driver based on how much he wanted me to tip him and what he thought was appropriate (and after agreeing that $3.00 was perfectly fair), the price for gas has really leveled around that amount for quite some time. Up a little bit, down a little bit, but no great increase or absurd nonsensical decrease. For quite a long time, since this cab hopping experience, how my mania plays a role in seeing and interpreting a greater purpose captures an extensive amount of my attention; especially, how I and my actions play into this greater purpose.

My last cab ride dropped me off at around 4 in the morning at the 5am bar, hoping that some of my co-workers were still around. The bar was empty. I was walking distance to my car. Hoping it hadn't been towed, I walked a quarter mile back to my car, parked in the valet spot with no ticket (clear sign that if you can act the part you are the part), and drove to my apartment ready for bed.

The next day I woke up scared. Did I still have a job? My parents knew that something had gone wrong. They made sure I was granted a mental leave of absence from work and I was welcome back when I was good and ready. After a couple weeks, I resumed work, and everything was brushed over and forgotten or at least ignored. People weren't really asking me any questions, so I felt no need to explain myself … business as usual.

The sports broadcasting job that I had been working at for almost two years to this point was unaware of my mental illness. Although, to get a mental leave of absence, HR had to be clued into my scenario, the rest of the office, including my best friends, had no clue that I was bipolar. This was a learning experience for me and a pretty tough one. It was hard hiding this factor from my co-workers. I feel if I was more open about this certain aspect of my life that plays a pretty big part of who I am, it would have been easier to cope with my feelings and also explain a lot of what I was dealing with. I know that the group I worked with would've been cool about my mental disorder. I learned from that job that I would never hide my disability at work ever again.

At the turn of the year it was clear that the company I was working for had no clear place for me. We parted ways (aka: officially, I was terminated) in early 2016. I had to restart my life, but more importantly, at least in my mind, I no longer worked with the girl I had fallen in love with. Losing the job was for the best. The only reason I could even cope working at the job was having the chance to see my office crush day in and day out. Getting fired helped me tell the girl how I felt about her. Now that we were no longer working together, I finally worked up enough courage to tell her how I really felt about her. After two years, it had to be pretty obvious. The timing wasn't right; with me it never is. Getting turned down by this girl after I was fired didn't really bother me. I was more hopeful than ever that it would work in my favor. Finally, I no longer worked with this girl, and I didn't have to worry about creating an awkward work environment for the both of us.

So I lost my job, my career. I had, seemingly, blown any chance I had with the girl I had spent probably the last year wholeheartedly in love with. What now? My answer … the only thing that was offering me any therapy or peace of mind. Drive. Driving kept my mind on and gave me the chance to simply think. With the radio on, doing endless laps on Lake Shore Drive, I felt free and comfortable, when really, I was feeling quite alone. Some people read books, play video games, watch TV; I roll my windows down, blast the radio, and escape.

Chapter 13
A Hobby Turned Addiction

Picked up seasonal work heading into the summer of 2016. Pretty much just started where I had left off and found work back at the local public course. Half my job was driving around on a big tractor cutting the fairway and listening to music so most of the time I felt right at home. My driving habit only worsened. I was addicted to the lights, the songs being played on the radio, the hats all over my route, and I had even started paying closer attention to the license plates of all the cars.

Don't kid yourself, I couldn't afford the habit. I was leaning on my parents; a pattern that I had become habitual and sad. Sad because I never took accountability for my own livelihood. I don't have an excuse, I just know that driving, listening to music, and watching the lights go on at night all over Chicago really helped me. On top of that, my mom and dad bought me an apartment of my own. Again, no excuse. Didn't earn the place through my own hard work. It was gifted to me. While working the next three years, I lived primarily off my parents. I learned later on what this actually meant to many different parties involved.

It's like I said earlier, once a strange or peculiar instance or co-incidence occurs, you can't stop looking for it over and over and others as well. You have no choice but to connect dots. Driving became so much a part of my life that I had begun paying atten-tion to detail along my loop. Now driving southbound to 31st, turning around and heading back to Bryn Mawr; rinse and repeat/hours and hours on end. What stuck out? What changed? What the hell kept me so captivated?

Dealing with manic depression you tend to live on the edge; you learn to find comfort there; it makes you check your own mortal-ity. They say *carpe diem*. Living on this precipice that so many of us find exhilarating, a ledge that most others can't get to, confirms without any doubt that you truly are taking it all on. I avoided a serious manic episode for years since pulling out of work in the summer of 2015, but hypomania became my preferred state of being. With a full-time job and another full-time job driving my car around Chicago, my sleep started getting stretched thin. Drugs played a part, but the driving alone got me in an elevated state. I told a doctor once, "Mania isn't thinking crazy thoughts; everybody thinks crazy thoughts -- mania is acting on those crazy thoughts." Driving around, I was thinking, but not acting. My mind would feel unbelievably activated; a total rush. I don't really know how to explain it other than that. It was very emotional, peaceful, and beautiful.

I can admit, I was running on a slippery slope. Besides the idea that I believed that the lights in the city were sending me signs, I looked for even more signs. I knew I was being watched carefully. I had piss spots. One right off the Bryn Mawr exit and the other at the turnaround at the 31st circle. Sure enough, the city put up "No Parking" signs in both my spots. I loved it! I knew they were watching me, and they were just putting up barriers to mess with my routine. I don't think they were trying to harm me. I think they were bored as hell having a fun time just messing with me. Everybody notices cops, but I started noticing even more. I knew I was being watched, that we can confirm by the "No Parking" signs, but how closely is up for debate. Hats were the next coincidence that kept me going. I was seeing hats all over the drive as if they were being planted. I believe that people lose their hats all the time out the window of their cars, but every time I saw a hat it felt like someone planted it there to say keep going … you're getting closer. Suddenly, I was cracking some puzzle. The driving was going to lead me to the answer.

Fired from a job and the distance between the girl I had a crush on was only growing. Absence makes the heart grow fonder. From what I heard, she was moving on her own path out of Chicago and out of my life. I had already poured my heart out to her, mostly through email. The first email I sent to her was a pretty standard love letter. I got no response. I sent her another email/love letter, but the second time I said what really needed to be said. No colloquial-type bullshit. Same result as the first love letter; none whatsoever. No rejection, but no response. Was it an eye-roll type response where what I said didn't even matter? Or was there more to it? I couldn't give up. I spent endless hours driving around the city of Chicago thinking about this chick.

Chapter 14
Desperate for Clues

We were officially living in different states, but I had to let her know that I wasn't calling it quits on my legitimate feelings for her. She never answers her phone or returns text, so I had to reach out to her some other way. I recalled a conversation I had with her one night at a bar explaining my four favorite colors. She liked how I had four favorite colors as it's basically just a way to not admit your actual favorite color. So I texted her. "Green" (one of my favorite colors). A prayer. You bet. I had nothing else. Had no clue if it would even mean anything to the girl. A long time had passed since we even talked. Maybe up to a year. I check my Instagram regularly enough and not two days since I had sent that text, perhaps a couple more, who's counting, she's in a picture on Instagram with two friends and their hair tips are all green. Am I being made fun of? Who cares? She's the one who took the time to make that photo happen. Are my eyes deceiving me? No. This chick really got her hair done up green. I took it as a sign. She's down to flirt on this level and Instagram is a medium we can use.

So I sat there. In my car driving around in circles thinking about the right approach. Instagram … a medium I generally ignore. I used the app from time to time, sure, but I am not exactly an actively involved user. I thought about how dating websites work. Swipe right and bam you're in. Instagram was no different as far as I could see. It was like the polite way to date, mingle, and scroll through pictures of hot chicks. The difference was, on Instagram nobody shows their cards. They're all looking at the pictures of the girls they like but they keep it coy and clever hoping it develops into the dm's as they call it. Forget that approach. If I was gonna use Instagram, it was for one purpose. Win this girl's attention for good. I was all in. The answer fell into my lap. I messed around with a couple photo shots with some clever lines but eventually I came up with the answer. The answer that was playing on my radio as I drove around Chicago thinking about this girl. All these endless number of songs; It's like giving a girl a mixtape when you like her. Except my mixtape was going to be broadcasted all over Instagram. Polite flirting, trying to gain a person's attention, get a like or two. Not what I was going for. Clear and obvious. Post this shit with no obvious intent but obeying the rules of Instagram; a clever approach to win a girl's heart and tell her exactly how you feel about her. An attempt to take things to the next level, but where or what that level was had no clear answer.

Things develop how they develop. I picked up a new hobby. Finding music of all variety started becoming my mission. For a while I was posting songs on Instagram that maintained a logical stream from one song to the next. Sure enough, I started posting songs on Instagram that I just liked … a lot of those songs expressed how I felt … and a lot of the times they related directly to the girl I was hopelessly reaching out to. My message was getting across. I felt it. Not only that, every once in a while, I got a clue in some form or another. She was keenly flirting back. I had to trust my instincts.

The driving got worse. By the summer of 2017, I was working part-time for my brother and hardly making it. I drove endlessly. I was in constant search for reassurance out on the road. Any little thing could have meaning. I was hardly working, but I was strung out. Even with little clues here and there, I needed more answers. Think outside the box I told myself. What's my next move? What can I do next to reach out to a girl who has been out of my life for over a year? I started racing cars on Lake Shore Drive. It got pretty dangerous weaving in and out of traffic. At one point, I hit 120 mph in the middle of the day going southbound right before my exit. I did everything I knew I could do and was left with nothing. I felt beaten.

Chapter 15
Willing to Die to Seek Answers

Mania, and especially hypomania, can be addictive. It's a rush that you can start looking for. All the signs I kept noticing while driving around the city pushed me into a mindset that I was seeking. Looking out for cues along my drive gave me hope that there was more out there; a bigger picture; answers; clues; all these things that helped me think I was on some sort of "right path." Some of it was made-up, no doubt. And I was smart enough to compartmentalize all of it. Analyze what was all in my head and what out there was just a little too coincidental. It wasn't one little trigger urging on my behavior. It was and became everything I saw and witnessed. I had a quote on my Facebook wall for a long time from Voltaire -- it went something like this: *Being crazy is the act of putting all your focus on one single thing or the act of putting your focus on everything.* If you look it up, you'll know he said it more eloquently than that, but, nevertheless, I was focusing on everything. Looking for signs everywhere I went and trying to organize the chaos. It was a recipe for disaster, especially being prone to psychosis and mania. The thing is, I loved it. I saw beauty in the world and opened up my mind to this world of chaos only to find purpose. Many of my drives in the confines of the city were filled with tears in my eyes as I felt the world calling to me even urging me on. The driving itself was dangerous as I began racing cars along Lake Shore Drive, and the cost of the driving was absurd. But it's where I found peace. Alone, radio on, windows down, turning the paved streets into my sea. Emotions would range from anger to ecstasy. I felt free and I knew there was hope. Hope because that's what I analyzed from all these non-existent signs that I was creating in my own head.

Every day was a little different. I didn't feel counted out. I lived for the rush of each day along my trail. Some days I would drive four hours. Some days I would drive 36 or more. I waited for the signs to control my feelings and the discourse of each day. It must have been around September of 2017 when the journey in my car took me for an unplanned trip.

In the middle of the day with the seasons changing (which of course was always scary because it meant another winter without a job and no prospects) I got lost with no intentions other than to keep an open mind. I went off my regular route on Lake Shore Drive. Following green lights and the blinkers of the cars in front of me I wound up in a part of Chicago I had never seen before. Somewhere around 87th and 76th, if that makes any sense (my memory on the exact location is hazy). I was on the wrong side of the block. The Hood. I was by far the minority on these streets. I had just lost a little weight and I was feeling myself just a little bit. It was time to test my street savviness. Getting killed was an option and I was in the right part of town to find that kind of trouble if I didn't come correct.

Why was I venturing into the "wrong side" of town? I needed answers. I had nowhere to turn. No one to talk to. Maybe gaining a new perspective from people I've never met could give me the sign I kept searching for.

Rolled up to three guys walking on the sidewalk. Rolled down my window. "Yo, you guys know where I can ball." Took these guys by a little bit of surprise. Had to explain to them that I meant basketball. Kind of a stereotypical racist assumption that these guys would know where a pick-up game was going on but it's probably better than asking for drugs. They helped me out. They gave me directions to a spot about a block and a half away right next to a gas station. Jokes on me, of course. The basketball court next to the gas station was a square vacant lot; probably about the size of a perfect Wiffle-ball field. Fenced in with some brush and garbage in the far-right corner. No hoops just fence and gravel.

Parked my car across the street next to the gas station. Left my keys in the car because I usually do anyway. This is my city and in my city my car is VIP (that's just how I feel, I hate locking things because it shows that I don't trust my fellow man). Crossed the street ready to hop the fence but lucked into an opening in the fence line. Got inside the square and just started cleaning up the trash and tree debris. Figured if I was gonna get anybody out playing ball with me I'd have to clean-up our court. Moved about three piles and sure enough it appeared: a 2-cm steel pipe, hollowed out in the middle, the exact length and pretty damn close weight of a baseball bat. Time to play.

I went around, corner to corner, hitting rocks. Swung both left and righty and was making decent contact each time. I wasn't having fun. I was blowing off a lot of steam. I was swinging over and over, corner after corner, rock after rock, getting more and more pissed off. Why? I was upset nobody was out there playing with me. I wasn't getting the answer I was really seeking. Went to the last corner and threw up a rock batting righty. Crack it perfectly. Hit it all the way to the outfield. It got a good bounce and rolled right out of the fence line. I just hit a home run. Threw the bat in the air and went back to my car. My keys were gone. Looked all over for them. Who cares? Didn't bother me. I had unfinished business. Went back into the field and just started running the bases. Ran around and around the corners of the field until my pants fell to my ankles and I was winded. Went back to my car and the keys were on my seat. Maybe I left them there or maybe not … didn't matter.

Had my keys, but I wasn't done. The anger was still there. I needed to do something. I needed to say what was really on my mind to the person that was constantly on my mind. I hadn't let her go. I couldn't. I won't. There was a gentleman pumping gas. I picked up my phone and typed what needed to be said. "Please find me and f@ck me, please." No way in hell I would ever send her that message. I went up to the guy pumping gas. "Sir, please help me." He was scared. I said, "I have this message on my phone … (I read him the message) … I want to give you my phone, you can either press send, delete the message, or throw the phone in the trash." He said he didn't want the phone. I asked him what I should do. He said, "Throw your phone in the garbage." So I threw it away right in the gas station trash can. Bye-bye iPhone 6.

Where was my mind at to have the gall to do something so

stupid? It's just like I wrote earlier; I was in search of perspective. I had been pretty damn attached to my phone for the past year, especially with Instagram; a medium that was keeping me in a hopeful but distant touch with the girl I was wrapped up in. If a doctor tells me to take all these meds because they will help me stay stable and feel good, then I don't have a problem listening to a stranger giving me advice to throw out my phone. It's a different kind of medicine, but maybe just the medicine I needed. I wasn't in my part of town; I was in the guy's part of town getting gas that day. If he says that I should throw my phone in the garbage, well then, when in Rome. My trip on the South Side was long from over. Still without an answer and with plenty of energy I made the area I got lost in aware of my presence. I tested my own street cred. I was lucky to be on my way home completely unscathed before nightfall. I went immediately to bed to reset and find stability.

I couldn't tell you how much time passed when I got back home. It wasn't too long. A few days, maybe. Hypomanic, for sure. Slipping into mania … pretty damn close. My brother caught me this time. He knew I needed to get one hell of a grip. He had a lot of questions … including what the hell could've possibly happened to my phone; nobody in my family could reach me. He had just gotten an upgrade and loaded my old phone's data, saved on his laptop, onto his old iPhone 6. I had a phone again. I got back online and got a hold of myself just in time. My actions might have shown that I had lost it, but I was making clear and cognitive decisions. I wouldn't have changed my actions in the past week, nor how I handled the situations I came across at all.

Chapter 16
A Mother's Concern

The bigger picture of life is something people with bipolar often struggle with and attempt to discover. I worked with a waitress later in life whose son was bipolar. She told me how hard it was to connect with him referring to a story about when he was five years old and the two of them were crossing the street and the waitresses' son looked up at her and asked, "What is all this about?" (referring to life and the world). I told her: I know … I understand completely … with people like us we tend to have a deep train of thought and spend our whole life searching to find answers; it's all part of the rush. It doesn't need to be a bad thing: It's not. Turning it up on the mean streets of the South Side, risking sliding into a manic episode, being reckless with my own well being, living on the precipice of life … I was searching for my own answers for, perhaps, a simple problem, but I was discovering bits and pieces of what makes it all fit together. I guess I was looking for the answer to my prayer in all the wrong places and in all the wrong ways, but I was loving the ride.

Thanksgiving 2017 came and went. I was stable but still driving. The only work I was doing was delivering flowers for a neighbor and friend and taking care of a puppy. I was running through money. Not only the vast majority of my bills, but gas for my car was all being paid for by my parents. I knew it was no way to live. I knew I had a driving problem. The problem I had was saving my life. I needed the driving addiction. I needed the time to sort out my emotions and escape to a place where I felt comfortable. I was worrying my mom.

December rolled around and the games with my parents officially began. A lot of the time people have their own problems in life, and they project their own problems onto you. Did I have any problems? No doubt about it. I had all kinds of problems: driving, drugs, career, friends. None of these things were in order.

My mind was clear. That trip to the South Side had come and passed. My hypomania cravings were not going to just disappear. They still exist today. That does not make me manic. Your own problems in life don't justify creating or manifesting the problem being my personal mental state. If something is really amiss, it will be hard to miss. If you start playing doctor because of suspicion, it can really be detrimental; it's an incredibly hard line to balance on -- when to help or when to breathe easy. Especially knowing how debilitating mania can become, can be, and is.

So my mom took all my medication out of my apartment, stole my car with the spare key, and decided that I needed to stay with her in my parents' apartment until I'm "better." Why would that ever be an acceptable answer? I have no idea. No way in hell was I going to accept that little proposal. Told my mom that if that is what she wants, then I'd rather check myself into a mental institution. I stormed out of her apartment and walked to Northwestern Hospital in downtown Chicago for a psychiatric evaluation.

I had been admitted to the psych ward on two different occasions up to this point. The first time absolutely destroyed me. It scraped away a lot of who I was up to that point. The only reason I ever rebounded, and trust me many people really never do … it's quite a shock to the system, is because of my family and closest friends. My family offered never-ending support and my closest friends never seemed to care. I could always be who I always had been with these two groups. Going back to college, facing what I faced head on, I did because I was headstrong. I knew I couldn't let that challenge beat me. Can't really say I won, but I did good enough, and that's enough of a win. The second time I was admitted to the psych ward was bullshit. I got drunk in public and made a big scene, so instead of throwing me in jail and giving me a laundry list of charges and fines, they admitted my dumb ass. But the third time was about to happen and I was clear and consciously attempting to get admitted because my mom was trying to take over my livelihood. Now I'm not stupid. My mom was using my mental illness as an excuse to monitor my life moving forward. That was her mistake. The truth was pretty simple. She just wanted me to get my life together. I don't fault her for that. I needed to. But the answer wasn't to start living with my parents and be surveyed by those two. What was the answer? No clue. If I knew that, I would have already had my life put together. I applied to jobs, entry level and minimum wage jobs alike. I wasn't getting any call backs. I knew it was a problem, but my mom was making it into a problem with my bipolar disorder and that is very, very wrong.

I showed up to Northwestern emergency room and asked to be admitted. This became a great learning experience. Room after room. Doctor after doctor. Mind test after mind test. I must have spent 12 hours receiving evaluation. As always, they ask if you are a harm to yourself or others. The answer was "No." What were all the doctors thinking? Why the hell is this guy here? At one point they put me in a room all alone. I started using the chair in the room to do sit-ups. Thirty seconds later a nurse comes into the room and takes away the chair. This was too funny. I was being watched. I went right up to the mirror in the room and put my finger straight on it (this was a way of seeing if it was a two-way mirror or not; it was). Right after I put my finger on the mirror one of the doctors' pops into the room and I move to the final hospital room/test. This is where they wait for as long as it takes until you fall asleep. After you fall asleep, they wait a certain amount of time -- the amount I do not know -- and then they wake you up for questioning. That way they get honest answers out of you because you tend to talk more, and more truthfully, when you're really tired and have just been woken up in the middle of your sleep.

So I fell asleep, they woke me up, and it was time to meet the decider. The decider is the head psychiatric doctor assigned to your case at the hospital. A little tired but clearly able to confirm my story from start to finish. The doctor in this case told me that she was against admitting me to a psych ward as she did not deem me manic in any way. However, because I was using the psych ward as a type of a sanctuary, she was willing to go against her better judgment as she found it in the best interest of me, the patient. An hour later, I'm being wheeled off on a hospital bed, tied down because that's what they do with mental patients, and brought to Methodist Hospital not too far from where I lived. I got to watch the whole process unfold at full mental capacity and I was having a great time. In the ambulance ride to the hospital, I had the two ambulance drivers play me some of the music they liked. I didn't really care for it, but who am I to tell these guys that they're listening to crappy music.

Admitted into Methodist Wing 5 South, I was about to encounter a psych ward visit with a totally level head; again, another big learning experience. It got old real fast. I wanted out almost immediately, but I knew I had to go through the motions. Nobody but the doctor assigned to my case at the mental institution really knew why I was there. So for all the social workers and nurses you encounter throughout the day and night, you're just another patient; there's no special treatment.

Chapter 17
Psych Ward Training

From the first day onward, I wasn't seeking help. I didn't really need to be there. It's funny, a little over a year ago, I got into a master's program at DePaul University in social work and counseling. I only signed up for one class to get my feet wet. I went to two classes and dropped out. It wasn't my scene. At the end of the day, I could do all this work, and pay large sums of money, for a master's degree that I truly believe I could've earned. But what was I getting out of it? They say everyone with bipolar disorder reacts to the mental illness differently. Every case is different for each person afflicted. This is true for most things across the board. When I dropped out of DePaul, I felt like I had a pretty good read on how to handle people and how to treat individuals on a case-by-case basis. It wasn't worth my effort for that piece of paper.

As a completely sane patient in the psych ward, I was in a unique position to help the other patients. Most of the people admitted to these places don't want to listen to the social workers or the nurses. They just don't relate. They have an outsider's perspective. I started going to group classes immediately. The first class, the social worker leading the group sat there doing her best to offer guidance and support. She was lost and out of her element. She didn't do anything wrong; she encouraged open dialogue and discourse and was trying to put a positive spin on things, but a lot of these patients really need to be checked. The social worker is almost never in a position to do that. But I was. I was in the same spot as every other patient in those group classes. My voice was louder than any social worker's voice. Patients are more willing to listen to advice or critique when it comes from their equal. People know that you're walking miles in the same shoes.

After one of my group classes, one of the social workers came up to me and started telling me that there are classes I can go to outside the hospital. I started telling her how I had already taken classes at DePaul. We talked a little longer and that's when we came to the goofy realization that she was talking about more group classes whereas I was talking about classes in social work at a university. Honestly, I can only imagine how difficult it is to work as a social worker at these hospitals, but I came to the conclusion that you can be way more beneficial to the other patients working as a patient yourself.

My Methodist 5 South visit was a psych ward training session. A lot of the inpatients come in with addiction problems. I figured out exactly how they were solving that problem. Sugar. With three meals a day, two coffee breaks, and late-night salami sandwiches, the patients in 5 South were being cut off whatever drugs they were on and stimulated with sugar. Sugar in the decaf coffee they drank; sugar in all the food we ate ... maple syrup, juice, and ice cream were served with breakfast, lunch, and dinner, respectively. Sure enough, you stop having to look at the clock come mealtime. You need that sugar fix and you line up at the door before the trays of food ever even show up. We had a quiet hour in the early afternoon. I would always request to use the shower at that time because I can't sit still in these places. In the shower I would do squats until I maxed out. My general routine was what I always do in these places. I would walk the hall; back and forth, back and forth. Like I said I can't sit still. A lot of the other patients, in all the psych ward visits I've had, end up copying me. It's the only way I know how to make the clock tick faster. I also learned how to trade food properly at mealtime. This hospital visit was unlike the other two I had been in beforehand. I was the minority in this place. I enjoyed being in that position. I wasn't going through any real hard shit, so I had my wits about me well enough to earn respect. Not only from other patients, but a lot of the senior staff as well.

My trip to Methodist 5 South was the first in a string of future hospital visits. The people you meet in these places are worth getting to know from whatever walks of life any of them are from. Everybody has a story and a struggle. Many are not worth talking to or remembering, but I learned that other patients can help you get through your visit as they're going through it with you as well. The doctor that was appointed to me was worth remembering as well.

After five or six days my visit ended. My mom met me at the hospital lobby. We had unfinished business. Who better to help mediate our problems with the actions that put me in Methodist than my own psychiatrist of twelve years. We went right to his office. Point counterpoint. I won. I got my house keys back and my car keys. The takeaway -- I figured out exactly how psych wards operated, what they were looking for, what they were watching, and how to act. It would come in handy.

Chapter 18
Betrayed

The winter dragged on. I was killing time until spring. Early in the winter of 2018, I was doing a bunch of flower deliveries. It was getting me through, but it wasn't work. I have no problem working. I have a good work ethic. My problems come when I'm not working. Free time gets me driving, gets me in my head, gets me off any type of realistic schedule. The winter was drifting away, and I had to figure out my job situation. Last summer I worked for my brother and that wasn't going to be an option again. Flower delivery after flower delivery and I kept driving all over the place in the northern suburbs. I kept having to take Golf Road. or ended up doing deliveries next to driving ranges or actual golf courses. It was a sign. I had to get back in the golf game. Delivered flowers up north and accidentally got lost. Wound up at the clubhouse at Bryn Mawr Country Club. Had to go in and ask for directions. Asked the best way to contact the superintendent as well. This was a private course, and something that might look good as I might have the opportunity to diversify my groundskeeper's background. Delivered the flowers, went back home, and put together my resume. Spring was near and the timing was perfect.

Walked into the maintenance shop with aviators on, asked for the superintendent, and had a job interview on the spot. Shook my new boss' hand as he told me he'd be calling me in a couple weeks, and I told him I'd be ready when he called. It was almost April and I felt pretty relieved. I finally had employment.

I just couldn't get that girl off my mind. Every once in a while, I'd shoot her a text knowing I'd get no response. Figured if it really was bugging her, she could just block me; and if she liked it, then I wasn't harming anyone. Her birthday was coming up. It had been a while since we had any type of back and forth. What could I do? Since we basically had a semblance of a relationship on Instagram, I decided I would unfollow her on her birthday.

My birthday was 6 months away to the day. I figured, even if she didn't notice I unfollowed her, come my birthday I would follow her again, and that way she would know I'm still thinking about her. It was 3rd grade bullshit, but I was okay with that. Better than nothing (I know it's so sad, but it gets better).

My mom's antics took a turn for the worst. I was promised a job in less than two weeks at a private golf course not far from where I lived and just outside the city limits on the northside of Chicago. Even though I was driving up to eight hours a day, perhaps more, I was prepared for the future, excited as well. All of the sudden, my doctor of over twelve years started acting unacceptably. He was calling me into his office to check-up on me every other day, maybe more. For over a week, I was going to his office and receiving scripts to have my blood levels checked on a constant basis. I might have had an abstract schedule with all the driving I was doing, but I was taking my medications daily. I should always be the one setting up my own psychiatric appointments … not my psychiatrist. I knew why he was so concerned. It was clear that my mom had my doctor's ear and attention. She was calling him because she herself was worried about me. Her worrying spread to my own doctor. They were communicating and coming to the determination that I was unstable. The diagnosis had no merit. My lifestyle was beyond obscure, but it did not and should not reflect on any conclusion about the possibility that I was mentally unstable. Moreover, my doctor shouldn't have been allowing my mom to control the discourse of our current proceedings. He shouldn't have been manipulated by her own analysis of my mental health. I wasn't even communicating with my mom at the time, and therefore, she could not have been knowledgeable of my mental health. If anything, my doctor should have been concerned about her more than me. It was a strange circumstance that angered me. I was angry at my doctor, but even more upset with what my mom was doing.

Just waiting for the call to start my new job, my doctor called me into his office for the last time. The meeting was just like all the meetings I had shown up for in the past two weeks. I had no idea why I was there I just knew that I felt good and that there was nothing else to talk about. He pleaded with me that I go to the emergency room and get a psychiatric evaluation. NO WAY. That's some bullshit. I was pissed. He insisted. A knock on his office door ten or fifteen minutes into the meeting unveiled my mom ready to drive me to Rush Hospital to get checked out. I went off at both of them. I agreed to go, but warned my mother that if we went, there was a good chance she would end up getting admitted. I knew far too well how these emergency room evaluations were done, I knew I was completely stable, and I knew all the right things to say. I figured I was going to be okay but warned that the conspiracy that my own doctor and mom had created in the past couple of weeks would be proven. I figured, even if I was the one going to get evaluated, my mom would be the one that would be looked at as unstable: I believed she was. We left my doctor's office for the last time and headed to the emergency room at Rush Hospital against my better judgment and all the fiber in my bones.

The evaluation had begun, and I was calm, relaxed, and knew exactly what I needed to say. The doctor's asked the questions that I had all the right answers to, and I knew that they were coming. "Do you consider yourself a harm to yourself or others" … "No, not one bit." The questioning moved forward slowly with my mom in the room. I was in the emergency room undergoing a psychiatric evaluation under the recommendation of a respected psychopharmacologist from their own hospital. The questions kept coming. It was clear that they couldn't find reason to admit me. Unfortunately, they were looking for more. They were looking for a reason. They had intent. Their intent was unfounded and unacceptable but stemmed from an uneasiness over letting me leave, ignoring the concern my own doctor -- one of their own -- had, as well as the concern of my own mother, present in the evaluation. If the closest people in my life believed me to be unstable, they didn't feel right ignoring those people. After all, I was the one already diagnosed with bipolar disorder, and therefore, I must be the one with problems. Downright unacceptable and completely and utterly morally wrong; perhaps unprofessional, as well, and borderline illegal.

The head of the psychiatric unit that day came into the picture for his own take on the proceeding examination. It was now his call what was to happen. He asked if he could talk to my mom and asked if he could question her and myself separately (in separate rooms). I had no problem with that. I figured anything she said couldn't possibly be used to determine my own mental stability. It wasn't her being examined. It was me. He talked to me, briefly. Asking many of the same questions I had already answered and getting calm coherent responses. He then went to speak with my mom. After their conversation, he came back in the room and filled me in on what my mom was so concerned about. He spoke of the driving problem I had and the stories that I had told my mom and family; things that had gone on or happened a long time ago; things that I had stopped. It was clear that my mom had fabricated my own stories, acting as if many of these things had been going on in the past couple of weeks. TOTAL LIES. He delivered the bad news. He came to the conclusion that it was best if I was admitted to a psychiatric hospital immediately. Without my permission, without just cause. My understanding of my own rights under the law was that I had to willingly admit myself. I didn't waste time. I knew there was no arguing the decision. I lost it. I did not threaten or act violently, but I screamed in anger. I was being sentenced to a mental institution; a place I knew to be damn well close to Hell. My rights were being ignored, and the hospital at Rush had been fooled, duped, and manipulated by my mom. I was administered a big shot of some anti-anxiety concoction in my right arm against my will. They had officially drugged me; a drug administered to knock me out.

Chapter 19
Psych Ward Training … Take Two

I woke up, I believe on a Saturday, in a place that had become far too familiar. I was garnished in hospital scrubs in a room similar in size to a college dorm room on a single bed with a bathroom off to the corner and a roommate not present in the moment I awoke. Immediately, I had an array of questions, but needed to first and foremost scope out my surroundings and quickly survey the lay of the land. I jumped right into my own psych ward mentality and began to walk the hallways. I was in the Lakeshore mental institution and it being a weekend, had to kill time until any question I had could really be answered. Doctors at these places don't work on the weekends and I would not be able to talk to my assigned doctor until Monday. Even if a patient signs a five-day (meaning that they are putting in their official request for release in five days), the weekend days do not count; it's only the business days that count toward one's time.

Lakeshore was different from any of the places I had been previously. This hospital was coed, like all the rest, but many of the patients were younger and much smarter and more relatable to me. This doesn't mean there were not people with other differences and of all different walks of life. It became clear, real quickly, however, that the stories of the patients in this place were worth finding out. Something could be learned from them that might be useful as long as I kept an open mind. For the first time, I could learn more about myself and my own situation as there were people here who were going through relatable circumstances.

I marched the halls and showed up to every group class right from the start. Those two vices were the only way to make the clock tick faster. I was out of my element as I had been admitted to the hospital against my will. I no longer knew my rights. Was I even allowed to sign a five-day? The situation was perplexing and exhausting to think about not only for me, but for the hospital staff as well. Nobody really knew the answer. It was clearly an unusual circumstance.

I met with my assigned doctor on Monday. He came off hard and tried to throw the book at me. I lit into his ass for five minutes. I questioned why I was there and everything about how I had ended up there. He wasn't ready for the patient he was just assigned. I had a ton of fight in me and I knew exactly what my situation was, what the hospital was looking for, what they were trying to prove and show me, and what I was ultimately responsible for in order to get out. I was ready to get out immediately and won my doctor's opinion of my situation over. He was on my side and would move forward doing his best to make sure my stay was as short as possible. I had taken him so off-guard because I had all of my own answers. I proved immediately that I understood my situation and had the answers to back up my own line of reasoning. So much so that he could do nothing more but to apologize and offer as much help with my case as he could. After enough time, it was clear that he was answering to somebody else. If he called the shots, I would have been released right then and there. After ten minutes in our first meeting, once it all got laid out on the table, my doctor and I talked about his family and I offered him advice about getting his kids into college. He took notes. He determined that the place I had found myself in was not the place I deserved to be.

There was more to discover, but I stayed alert to my own circumstances. I did not assume anything. Until I was given an exact day and time of release by my doctor, I could take nothing for granted. Up the hallway and back down the hallway all day every day. Trying my best to only ask questions about my peculiar circumstance when appropriate. Again, nobody in charge knew the answer to the right way of confronting my stay. I had to trust that the doctor was going to get me out of this place in due time but knew I didn't necessarily have any way of affecting how much longer my visit would last.

Group classes and the time I spent with the other patients at this particular institution was ultimately rewarding. The core group that I spent time with and encountered at daily group classes was more than fun; it became an eye-opening and enlightening experience. Mostly peers, perhaps some years younger than me, but quite intelligent. Group classes, even with trivial objectives or discussion assignments, were mostly spent with this core group of peers. It was like spending time learning from one another with a group that was so well-informed that I believe I was spending time with elite minds, perhaps more elite than the minds I encountered at college. Our stories meshed together. All of us were confused about our own situation. We all had the ability to shed light, directly or indirectly, on each of our own personal journeys, and the journey people with our condition have had to deal with and have encountered. We quickly formed a bond and enjoyed one another's company. It made our drudging stay in this place worthwhile, even when most of us knew we didn't deserve the time. We were all placed here because of the condition we had, and were unjustly judged by others, because they didn't understand and couldn't explain the type of people we should have no shame in being.

My time of release came by the end of the week. I was getting out at noon on, I believe, the first Thursday or Friday in that first week. I had made it and had gotten a new and important lesson on how mental institutions function. The experience would yield importance. The whole stay was so messed up, so unjust, and so dysfunctional, that my exit from the hospital explained it all. After they injected me at Rush Hospital with a large dose of anti-anxiety medication, I passed out and woke up in Lakeshore mental institution. Not only did they not receive my signature of approval in the process, but, while I was passed out, they stripped me of my clothes and tossed my body on a bed in the new facility. With no record of my willingness to be admitted, they had also lost my clothes and shoes. I called my brother to come and pick me up at the time they agreed to release me: 12:00. It was 12:10 and my brother was waiting out front. I called him at 12:10 to make sure he was there. He said he had been waiting patiently for the last fifteen minutes. I walked into the mess hall where all the social workers were administering lunch for the other patients. There was nobody at the front where the nurses and social workers usually convened. I yelled boisterously, "My brother is out front, we are no longer on my time." Action took place immediately. The social workers were completely on my side. I had been here far too long. The doctor who was supposed to collect me and walk me out was unacceptably late. "Where are your clothes?" one of the workers asked … "I have no clue" … "Well, don't you need shoes?" … "You don't seem to have those either and I simply don't care. I just want to leave." The answer was accepted. Doctor or no doctor, they were getting me out the front door. The elevator door was opened for me. We went down to the first-floor lobby. The elevator door opened, and my doctor was walking in. I didn't even acknowledge him. The social worker taking me down the elevator told the doctor that she had the release paperwork and that my time here was over. In hospital scrubs and hospital socks, I walked out the front door to freedom. The first time I had been outside in six days. I casually got in my brother's car and drove off.

Of course, just as I had been worrying about, the phone call to start my new job had been made while I was at Lakeshore. It wasn't too late. I immediately phoned my future boss and was starting early Monday morning. I wasn't nervous knowing full well what I was getting into and that I was fully qualified. Working maintenance at golf courses is grueling manual labor work and tough enough on anyone's lifestyle as work begins before the sun comes up. Finally, I had a job again and was keeping an open mind about turning this type of work into a career. Not only that, I was beginning work at a private course; even if I wasn't making as much, I was jumping into something that was ultimately enhancing my resume.

Chapter 20
Finding My Own Value

Ever since being first diagnosed with bipolar disorder at age twenty and being put on all different types of medication, I was noticeably overweight. Initially, I had gained up to seventy pounds. Losing weight was always at the forefront of my mind, but I realized it was much harder than I had ever thought imaginable. Within the first week at my new job, I realized that this was a clear chance to drop serious weight. Eight hours a day of manual labor would turn out to be great exercise and just the type of boot camp I needed. Not only that and even though it took a month before my body adjusted to the work, I liked being outside in the sun, sweating and kicking ass.

Work at the golf course was being balanced appropriately with my driving addiction. It was going just fine except I was having trouble dealing with my boss. I got along great with the entire staff and accepted the fact that the job was tough with minimal pay. I showed up everyday happy to be working at a golf course and enjoying the beautiful surroundings of what had become my office. The superintendent drove me mad. He was never relaxed and clearly unhappy. Even on an unbelievable sunny day on a gorgeous private golf club, my boss was always stressed out. They say, don't forget to stop and smell the roses. This guy was seemingly incapable of doing so. I understand a lot of things constantly needed to be thought about and taken care of. There was always a lot on this guy's plate. But he needed to take a deep breath and look at the bigger picture every once in a while. We were surrounded by beauty. His stress was contagious. Everyone on the staff felt the weight of his stress. He was projecting it on all of us every day in every encounter anyone had with him. I couldn't take it anymore. We were just over halfway through the season, and I could no longer allow this guy to affect my personal happiness and demeanor. I wasn't being paid enough to have to let the stress eat at me once I had punched out for the day.

For two weeks I plotted my future plans. I put in for a couple days of time off to head out to my family's cottage in Michigan. Going into the vacation, I knew of a course out there that was beyond private. I had full intention of applying to work at the course or, at least, put in an application for employment. I knew I was qualified, and hoped they were willing to take on another staff member on the grounds crew, guaranteeing I would require little training and would be completely plug and play.

On the second day of my four-day vacation, I walked into the maintenance headquarters with my resume. I got the application in my hand, went home and filled it out, and showed back up to the course. I talked to the superintendent long enough to show him that I knew what I was talking about, and he gave me great hope that he was willing to hire me immediately. I drove back to Chicago hoping I would get a call sooner rather than later.

On my first day back at work, Monday, my future boss called me at lunch time and asked how soon I could start. I had to pack up my things in Chicago, quit my current job, and tie-up some loose ends. I told him I'd be ready to work by Thursday. I wasted no time. Before the end of lunch, I quit and never looked back.

Taking the job out in Michigan turned out to be one of the better decisions I've ever made. Undoubtedly, I left my at-will job in Chicago without a two weeks' notice. Was this wrong? Who cares. I didn't want to work there anymore and found a better job with more pay elsewhere. It was the right move for me. Jobs don't give you a two-week notice when they fire you. In a way, I was firing my old job and felt no need to put in two more weeks at a place where I was unhappy. My new job out in Michigan was exactly as I expected and that my employer was counting on. I had things to learn, but I was mostly plug and play. I knew my way around the shop, I knew how to use the equipment, and I could meet expectations.

Chapter 21
Unchartered Territory

My time in Michigan was a needed change, and the group I worked with from top-to-bottom taught me how much I truly needed to know, and question, as I continued to become a top-tier grounds crew worker. More importantly, this new group shared my out of work interests. We spent our mornings taking care of an exclusive private course and spent the afternoon golfing together at the cheapest local public course. We spent our nights blowing off steam hoping we would be sober enough to take care of business starting early the next morning. It was a work hard/play hard group, and I could hang. I loved every minute. The crew was small and tight knit, but I quickly became treated like family. I was an outsider that earned enough respect to be part of their team.

The driving continued even in my new surroundings. Up and down the roads I went during much of my free time. The girl I had fallen in love with was still on my mind. Even with zero communication I hadn't lost faith that she was the one for me. My initial plan was still in place. I intended to friend the girl in question on my birthday, October 1st. The date was nearing. Would she accept? Would she get the message? I didn't have the answers; just a prayer that the move would be well-received.

I went out to Michigan with about two months of bipolar medication. I was running out. It had potential to become a problem. I drove up to Traverse City in search of a doctor to write me new scripts. I wasn't juggling this very well. With all the driving, with this girl on my mind, with my new job, and with my new social life hanging out with my coworkers, I stopped caring. Things were going so well that I believed running out of medication wasn't going to be a problem. I tricked myself into believing I didn't need them for the rest of the time I was up there. The season was nearing conclusion, and I would be able to get back on my med regime once I was back in Chicago. I took the risk because of how great

I felt. Work was good, I was playing a lot of golf, I was having fun outside of work, I had lost over thirty pounds throughout the course of the summer, and I felt mentally sound. Nothing could throw me off, not even the absence of medication. After being off my meds for a few weeks I started to believe I didn't even need them. I no longer had any intention to seek refills before the season was over and it was time to go back home to Chicago.

My birthday finally came around. I re-followed the girl on Instagram. She promptly accepted the follow request. It was a funny and peculiar way of reaching out, I know. It didn't really mean anything, but it showed her that I was still thinking about her. It was all I had left even if it offered no real answers. Roughly two weeks went by. I was completely out of medication. I had to do more, but what. Things had slowed down at work and the season was turning over. It was getting colder, and I wasn't needed any longer. I put in my two weeks having fulfilled my obligation with all the intention in the world of finishing strong.

I missed the city and was beginning to really lose my cool. In my time out in Michigan I had begun drinking alcohol for the first time in six years. I was doing so responsibly, and it was not something that was affecting my work or my habit of driving in any way, shape, or form. I felt alive. I was getting this rush that I was really living again. I was excited about the experience I had gained working at the Michigan course. I was searching for a way to find the same work elsewhere. I reached out to places in New Zealand.

I couldn't deal with re-establishing any type of Instagram relationship with the girl that had just accepted my follow request. I needed to change the game. I needed to do something that sent her a message of how I really felt. I used Instagram to reach out to this girl, but, in all honesty, I wasn't using it for any other reason. I took the next appropriate action. I unfollowed every single one of my friends except her. She became the only person I followed. I figured this was the best way to go about showing my true feelings and intentions. Would she pick up on the move? Who knows.

I had made it to my last week of work. Without my medication, sleep had become harder and harder to find. I was running on empty and pretty strung out. I was driving non-stop; almost around the clock. I would get out of work, get in my car, and drive almost until I was due to punch in at work the next day. After work on Wednesday, I lost just enough control to make a couple of decisions that were against all my better judgment. I was invited over to my mechanics house to hang out late in the evening. He wasn't there when I showed up. I didn't show up empty-handed. I came with a few six packs of an assortment of beer. I knew I needed sleep and I intended to party with my favorite co-worker until I passed out. I intended to use alcohol to self-medicate as I was running out of any better answer; above all else, I knew I needed to find a way to get to bed.

Chapter 22
God on My Side

I parked my car at the mechanic's house and began the party in his yard without him. I turned up the radio in my car, opened up the doors, and lost control. I put down every beer I purchased pretty damn quickly. I threw up twice. Was I drunk? Probably not as the alcohol didn't really stay down. The mechanic's truck was parked less than 15 feet from my car. I hopped in the driver's seat. I found the keys. I had a hundred dollars in my pocket and nothing to lose. I wasted no time deciding to turn on the truck and head straight to the casino about 40 minutes away.

Things had yet to take a turn for the worst and I made it to the casino unscathed. I knew exactly that I was going to do with my hundred-dollar bill. I didn't park in a parking spot, as there was no chance I was going to be there long. I stopped the truck at the front of the casino's doors, threw it in park, and left the keys in the ignition. Strolled right in and found the roulette table. Put a hundred on red and waited for the result. In no more than one minute, I had doubled up. I cashed in my chips and headed back to the stolen truck. I wasn't thinking about being pulled over or any type of possibility of anything going wrong. I was flying high. My only concern was finding what radio station I wanted to listen to on my drive back to the mechanic's house. I pulled into his driveway, put the truck in park, placed the keys where I found them, and stepped out. What a rush. I saw the lights in the house on, so I invited myself inside. My mechanic came out of his bedroom with his new girlfriend with questions clearly on his mind. His girlfriend left the house immediately. I spent the next two hours sharing stories with my boss whose car I had just stolen. He was concerned about me, but didn't care otherwise. He wasn't mad one bit. He could have easily called the cops. He didn't even flinch. What a guy. The whole thing brought us closer than ever before.

My night was long from over, but my time working at the golf course would turn out to have an abrupt and unintended conclusion. I finished shooting the shit with my mechanic and jumped back in my own vehicle. I drove to a different casino an hour away in another direction. The casino had a poker room and I had two hundred dollars for a buy-in. I'm good at cards and sat at one of the two tables that had clear action. The other table only had three people while the table I sat at was full. As soon as I sat down, I knew I had no fair shot at making much money. The area was small enough that on a random Wednesday night in October there was more than a good chance that these guys were all regulars. When a new guy shows up at a table like this, they work together to take that guy for everything he's got. If I wanted to make any serious coin, I would have to spend quite a bit of time grinding with the odds stacked against me the entire way through. I drove all the way out to Traverse City to play cards and didn't want to go home right away. I played every hand no matter what the initial raise. The button had gone around about one time and I was down to just a little over a hundred dollars. I hadn't hit a single flop and I wasn't getting any great hands. Still I had earned a little bit of respect from the table by the way I acted and played. Even if they were trying to take my money, I was okay to play with this crew of regulars. Finally, I made my move after one of the flops. I only had a pair of sevens with an ace kicker, but it was time to try my luck. I had no other choice but to go all-in hoping to get folds all around. Unfortunately, I picked a bad spot to go for the small pot, and these guys all had plenty of money in front of them to draw against my hand; my hundred dollars didn't intimidate anyone at the table. Long story short, I lost the hand but watched one of the greatest hands unfold in front of me. Even better, I called the whole thing out while the betting was still going on. I knew what every player in the hand had and needed to win. I lost the last of my money and excused myself from the table. Every player was in awe of my ability to read the whole thing right from the flop. The drive out to the casino only heightened the rush I was on.

I got back into town and back home safe. I needed to sleep. I had work in about five hours. There are countless times, manic, hypomanic, or completely stable, where I know before I go to bed that falling asleep was not going to happen. I had been awake for over forty hours, but this was one of those times. When this happens, you have two options: Lay in bed, eyes closed or open, motionless, until you're supposed to get up and go about your business or accept that you're incapable of falling asleep and do something productive for the time that you're awake. I walked into my house, looked around, and walked right back to my car. No chance I was going to be able to shut down before work. Even if I did, I would end up with only a couple hours of sleep at most and go into work utterly exhausted. I headed away from town in the direction of Chicago. About twenty minutes away from home, I checked out my phone. I went on Instagram. Since I had narrowed down who I was following to one person, I was still getting plenty of random people's pictures. I found this strange. It only got stranger. All of the sudden, I was following twenty-three people. One of those people was the girl I liked, but the rest of the people were quite a random assortment. Most were people in my past and a few here and there I did not recognize. My phone app had quite clearly been tampered with. I checked my phone again, and a message popped up on the screen. "Pops is ready to play ball." This was enough of a message for me. I didn't look back. I was headed to Chicago. Forget those last two days of work.

The drive back to the city was around five and a half hours and was not without some crazy moments. I made the left turn onto the main highway that leads out of the State of Michigan. Quickly on the highway, I got a little sleepy and swerved ever so slightly to my left. I caught myself before exiting my own lane. VRoom VRoom. Three cars whipped in front of me. It was a clear race move. These three cars were clearly driving with me waiting for any kind of slip up I might have. I responded accordingly. I slammed on the gas and let the race continue. We were all weaving on the highway vying for position. We fell in line. I didn't have the faster car and knew my limits. The race only lasted thirty seconds, and I fell in second place. The escort I had out of Michigan did their part to wake me up. I don't know who was behind those three cars, but they had their eye on me. No big deal; it was clear that they were there to help. I made it to Chicago just before sunrise. The lights on the buildings were still shining bright pink, but daylight was looming. I couldn't help myself. I was back in the city and I had to let my presence known. I immediately hit Lake Shore Drive with authority. I raced northbound on full tilt back to my apartment. Eventually, I got back to my bed safe and sound ready to crash hard.

Chapter 23
False Security

Upon arriving in Chicago, the next month and a half of my life would become a time that nobody could ever be prepared for. All my suspicions about every little thing I had postulated were about to be confirmed. Of course, I would end up being left with no proof, but the affirmation was a relief. Still operating off my meds, I was avoiding slipping into mania, but I was constantly in and out of a hypomanic state.

I had just worked seven tough months at two different private courses in the country. I did good work. I had lost more weight than I had ever lost since I was twenty years old (over 12 years). I had a new body and a verified skill as a grounds crew member. I felt a great sense of achievement. I was also unjustly complacent. Sure, I deserved some time to decompress, but I wasn't looking for work at all. My personal funds would not last too much longer, and sadly I was satisfied being supported by my parents. It was the wrong attitude. I had this feeling that I had made it. I took my eye off the prize and forgot to focus on taking care of myself. This would turn out to be disastrous as time moved forward.

My brother had just moved to a new apartment downtown, and I spent most of my time away from driving hanging out with him and his whole scene. Sure enough, poker became the name of the game. My brother had linked up with a few others to start an underground poker room. Nothing too crazy. Just one table at a time at different locations with a young group that had the ability to throw around some serious cash. I began to hang out at many of the events. I didn't have the money to play, but I liked cards and enjoyed watching.

On my first night surveying one of the games, I was welcomed openly by one of the players at the table. I had played cards against him in my brother's previous building's social event. I crashed the party and took over the poker table the first time I met this guy. He recognized me as a good card player, and, even as a spectator at this new underground scene, this guy let the other players know I was cool and that they were lucky I didn't have chips in front of me.

I would come to find out just how small the world really is associating in this new crowd. Within the first three nights of becoming acquainted with this new group of people, my life was blown wide open. I only went to the underground poker games with my brother. He was playing and was my ticket in. Recognized by the one guy I mentioned earlier gave me enough credibility in the group that nobody questioned who the hell I was. Even crazier, many people who showed up started to believe that I was the one in charge of this whole underground poker network.

My first time involved, the game was held in the same building my brother was in, except on the top floor. I might not have been playing, but I was looking out at the other players making my own reads. The shit that was going on was illegal, and I was paying attention for any cop-like suspicious behavior. Didn't take long before I got uneasy about one guy in particular. Another guy at the table was making the same read as me. He played it cooler than I could've ever tried. He started acting like a cop himself. Of course, I became uneasy about both him and the other guy already under suspicion. I wasn't sticking around for any sort of sting. I made my move to get out of Dodge. I had no money at the table anyway, but I made enough of a scene before I left the room to alert any of the other players at the table, including my own brother, to proceed with caution because I made the read that the table was hot.

Less than a week later, I made an appearance to the same apartment for another cash game with many of the same group of players. Again, I was only an on-looker. Nobody mentioned the other night where I sounded the alarms. The vibe was that they appreciated that I was around looking out for that kind of thing. Right when I showed up, the guy I was originally uneasy about got up from the table and left for the night. I think I was right about that guy. Not only that, but I think I blew his cover. That was the last I saw of that guy. He talked too much while playing cards anyway. Some kind of know-it-all. I don't like those types. The other guy that was acting like a cop was at the table. I still had my suspicions about the guy and kept my guard up. I wasn't seeing any of these guys' hands, but I was watching the whole thing. This guy was one of the better players at the table. He wasn't a talker either. I started to loosen up as it became apparent that most of the players that night were familiar with the crew in the room. The night slowly came to an end and most people in the room had left. The guy I thought might also be a cop stood up in front of me and brushed back his hair. I couldn't believe it. I immediately spoke the guy's name out loud. He was a good friend of mine way back in high school, and I just finally recognized him.

My next time at the card table said it all. Again, I went with my brother. Mostly the same crowd. My old friend from high school was back. He wasn't using his real name and I had no intention of blowing up his spot. We both acted, perhaps more friendly, but without bringing up the past we had with one another in front of the people in the room. Quickly, I found out that the kid who made sure I was respected in the room and who knew, firsthand, that I could play cards was close friends with my boy from high school. They were a crew. The kid was the only person in the room that knew me, and his boy had history. Of course, a room full of guys playing poker, stories were shared. I paid little attention to any of the stories until my attention to one of the stories was requested, to say the least.

Chapter 24
The Crazy Puzzle Starting to Make Sense

The kid who made sure I was welcomed to events, the kid who I had bested not once, but twice, at a more casual card table, but more importantly, the kid who was a good friend, if not best friends with my boy from high school, wanted, nay needed, to tell me a story. It was important to him that I heard the story; forget the other players at the table. This story was for me. He said, "Will, I got to tell you this story … you have to listen. I want to tell this story because I need to know if I should feel bad … if I did something wrong … if someone finds out about the story I'm about to tell and they are angry or pissed at me." "Okay." I smiled. "Get on with the story," having no clue what the story could be, just knowing that somehow this story was relevant to me, and I was clearly the one, if anyone, that could possibly be upset at this kid, who I had no reason but to like since meeting for the first time less than a month ago.

The story made me one of the happiest men on earth. It was all about a time, less than a year ago, that him and my boy from high school had shared together in Vegas. Turns out that the two of them, high-rollers that they are, linked up with a couple women one night when they were out-and-about. They ended up with two women in one hotel room in Sin City. They're my age (low 30's). Things being what they are, they started to make out with the two girls. My boy from high school with one of the girls and this other guy with the other. Suddenly, the girls left the bedroom of the hotel room and had a quick meeting in the bathroom. They came back out, and it was decided before the casual hooking up turned into a sexual act that they felt the need to switch who they were paired with. Enough clues were explained about the ongoing proceeding that continued that night in Vegas, that I was no longer in the dark about why this kid wanted me to hear the story. He made it clear not only who the girl he was left with that night, but, more importantly, he relayed the message in a way that was clear to pick up on. This girl considered herself taken. This kid gave me the first message in over two years that she felt taken by me. Why else would this kid be telling me this story asking me if I would hold it against him? So he told the whole story and asked if he did anything wrong. I answered his question with a question. "Was the ratio right?" shrugging the story off. My boy from high school loved the response. He was laughing and nodding in approval.

If I wasn't already feeling on top of the world, this story put me there. Finally, evidence, abstract as it was, that the girl I was in love with considered me to be her man. It wasn't a stretch. That story was deliberately delivered to me. By her, of course not, but received nevertheless. I just got shot with the jolt of confidence I needed, wanted, and deserved. I didn't have to figure out my next course of action. I didn't have to reach out to this girl any longer. I was delivered a message that she and I were on the same page. We both saw one another to be in each other's future; we just needed that future to unfold naturally and eventually.

Chapter 25
Put on Trial

I've been sharing many stories with you, so far. Some of the stories you may believe and others you may assume to be fabricated. The feelings from these stories, real or imaginary, are undoubtedly, like the stories themselves, quite real. It is important for you to understand, going into my next story, that you understand people who are bipolar; people who deal with mania; people in this case that experience psychotic breaks, usually tend to interpret what's happening around them incorrectly. They make an assumption about what they saw or what someone said to them. They end up processing what's going on in the world around them inaccurately. It can greatly affect their ability to remain stable and their ability to avoid any length of psychosis. People who have bipolar disorder have the ability to lie and make shit up just like anyone else. You should know, what they're making up, only makes them a liar. What they are willing to lie about sure as hell can come back to affect their own mental state. What's important to take away from all this is that the story I'm about to share with you is not something I believe to be true, because I'm a psychiatric patient off my meds and am therefore manifesting events. If you believe my next story is a manifestation, fine. Then I'm a liar. But please do not come to any conclusion that the story, or any of my stories, are thought of and believed by me because I have bipolar disorder.

THE LOBBY INQUISITION

We were approaching Thanksgiving 2018. I was still thinking and going about my business shortsightedly. I had an extremely small amount of money in my bank account, and I had no plans to find work. I was completely stable. I wasn't taking my bipolar medication regularly enough that it could be considered effective. I was

on a set schedule; I was getting plenty enough sleep on a daily basis (usually the biggest sign that I am having trouble). My driving
addiction was still affecting my life, but even that was being done
on more of a schedule. Drugs were in play. Despite any doubt, I
was functioning at an adequate cognitive level. I felt good and my
brain was good.

Had to be the middle of the day ... maybe even early in the
morning. I had taken the "L" to my brother's apartment to hang
out. As usual, I had my earphones in and was listening to music.
I took a seat in the lobby of my brother's building with the intention to wait for my brother to wake-up so I could head up to his
apartment. The lobby in his building was huge. There were seats
at the far end of the lobby, way across from the front desk. I took
a seat and began to witness an incredible proceeding.

I sat facing the front desk of the lobby. The head lobby lady
was on duty. At least twenty yards of marble floor separated the
two of us. With one eye on my phone's playlist and the other eye
on my surroundings, I watched the scene unfold in front of me.

Young man enters the scene from the left. He approaches the
desk of the lobby lady and talks briefly with the lobby lady. He
leaves. Different young man enters the scene from the right and
approaches the desk of the lobby lady. More words were spoken
briefly, but at longer length. The young man exits. The scene has
my full attention. My left ear no longer had an earphone in it. My
right ear did, but the music was turned down. I did not want to
give off the appearance that what I was witnessing affected my
demeanor. It didn't take long for me to pick up on. I was in the
middle of some kind of court hearing and I wasn't just a bystand-
er ... I was the topic of the ongoing dialogue.

The lobby lady, aka the judge, didn't waste time blowing up the
covert proceeding. She recognized quickly that I was clued into
whatever was going on. She picked up the phone, "Ya, he knows
(talking about me), he knows he's on trial ... we're just going to
go on with it." She hung up the phone. I was no longer listening
to music. My phone had turned off, out of battery. My mind, my
reaction, my body language, I was on board. I wasn't freaking out

or one bit surprised. I sat there, on some sort of trial, slouching in my chair, ready for exactly what was to come.

How could I not be all kinds of shocked at what I just heard, at what was clearly unfolding right in front of me, how could I be acting so nonchalantly at this entire event? To understand the answer is to understand what got me to this point. Yes, I've done and been through some pretty crazy shit. Yes, my actions, especially with all the driving I've done, has gotten me noticed (by who or what I have no clue). These two things we, or at least I, know to be true. Is there something else, something I'm not telling you? People don't just get put on some ad-lib trial some morning in the lobby of a building; How could you be ready for that kind of thing? Moreover, how could you even begin to have expected it? The answer, at least, the short answer, lies in my phone. I've had a new iPhone, previously owned by my brother, since I threw my last one out on the South Side. I still have it today. It has a peculiar battery problem. Anyone clued-in would tell you that I just have a dysfunctional battery. The truth: the battery on my phone is being controlled. Depending on my actions, I will or will not have battery life. The battery life jumps up and down critiquing things I say and do. Why was I more than ready for this lobby inquisition? Maybe too crazy for anyone to believe, but simply not crazy considering all the shit that's always coincidentally happening in my life. It just seemed like the next logical step/or thing to happen.

So with this phone conspiracy theory aside, as I expect absolutely no one to understand or believe, the question becomes -- *What are you being put on trial in the middle of a lobby hotel room for?* The good news, I wasn't going to be guilty of anything. I faced no jail time. This trial was to discuss or come to terms over my future marital terms. It was mostly a prenuptial arrangement. There were other things on the line, but the judge of the hearing could speak to those things more than me. Those things were out of my hands.

With me across the room doing my best to listen in on what the hell could possibly be said, I approached the bench. Both lawyers were talking things out with the judge. The lawyer coming from the left side of the room, supposedly on my side, walked away.

The judge acknowledged my presence and simply said, "Relax, we're on your side; we're helping you." This was all well and good, but I just asked if she could charge my phone. She rolled her eyes and took my phone. My thought, especially now knowing that the judge was on my side, was you play courtroom and I'll play building patron who wants to get his phone charged.

It was amazing to watch the whole thing unfold. My lawyer or representation, or however you want to classify the guy coming from the left side of the room, stopped making any appearances. The other lawyer was pleading the case at hand. Now on record, I have no idea who was behind the lawyer from the right. Was he representing the girl of my dreams? Supposedly. But it should be noted, and it was understood on my part, that the prenuptial hearing that was taking place was happening because of other factors and people in the girl's life that felt as though they needed to set terms.

Things were being hashed out. Questions were getting answered. I approached the judge's desk at the front of the room. I asked for my phone back. The judge/lobby lady took my phone off the charger and looked at the screen before handing it back. "We're giving you 13%," holding the phone out for me to grab. Her word choice was no accident. In the midst of the proceeding I wanted to make a point clear. The best way to go about this was to send a text; a text to my mom but intended to establish the grounds of my own personal autonomy. I was clarifying that I acted alone and on my own behalf. I'm sure this was clear and known, but I wanted to drive home that notion because it became even more clear that the other side was not acting under that criteria. My 13% was quickly down to 1% and I approached the front to ask for my phone to be plugged back in. The judge read my text. "Perfect," she retorted out loud to herself. She and I were on the same page and she knew that I was compartmentalizing the proceeding correctly.

Things went too far. My net worth got questioned. The other side resorted to the importance of their wallet. The size of their wallet set the groundwork for their argument and their vision of marital guidelines. Forget signing something that determined that her money or family's money could never be mine or in my control. That was never even an offer. Instead, I was to take employment in the family business. I was required to work the rest of my life. It's laughable. In order to marry this girl, I would have to sign up for indentured servitude. The terms were non-negotiable. The good part is I didn't have to say anything. I didn't have to read through anything. I didn't have to discover these terms on my own or hire a lawyer to explain these terms in some sort of made-up document to me. I had some sort of judge hearing these demands and getting pissed for me. Totally on my side through the entire thing and great representation. She halted the other side's strategy as quickly as it developed.

I approached the bench for the last time. I'm not sure if there was anything still left to negotiate. From what I could pick up, hearing only one end of the telephone calls, it didn't look like we had reached terms on future marital bliss between the girl I loved and myself. She still apparently had one last question. "Numbers?" The lawyer from the right asked right as I went to ask for my phone back. I got my phone back and the lobby inquisition was over. I was still waiting on my brother. Finally, my brother gave the word to the lobby lady, former judge, that I could make my way up to his apartment. Before I went up, I approached the lobby lady, and I got in my last words, "I must not know my Deuteronomies," I said, befuddled.

I went on the rest of the day, business as usual, but as time moved forward, I slowly fell apart. One major symptom that people with bipolar disorder experience is this notion of grandiosity. We start drawing conclusions that our own personal existence plays a greater role or paramount role in society and/or the future of humanity. I kept my mouth shut on all accounts after the lobby inquisition. I knew what went on that day was far-fetched and completely unbelievable. It never became my goal to dig for evidence or acknowledgement that it all happened. I pretended it didn't. I was happy to know that the girl was in love with me enough to discuss the next step, marriage. It's hard to say how much time went by after what happened in the lobby of my brother's building before I fell into seclusion. It couldn't have been more than a few weeks. I think it began just before Thanksgiving that year. All I know is I didn't make it far into December before I had completely lost my mind.

Chapter 26
Mania Stems from Isolation

My life came to a disastrous halt. I felt like I had completed something I had not. I was lulled into a false sense of accomplishment and state of being. It was just a matter of time before I would be pulled from the reality of the life I was in and my new life would be revealed and presented. I escaped to the bedroom of my apartment and waited patiently. Far removed from medication, ignoring the bills I had to pay, delusion set in. I was carrying on conversations with myself, talking to the television, and creating an alternate reality. I had cut myself out from the outside world for weeks on end.

I jumped right into mania. Not only was I making all kinds of connections in my mind that had no merit, but I was acting irrationally. I didn't take the result of the lobby inquisition the right way. I thought the girl and I were closer now more than ever before. Perhaps things between the two of us were still very much salvageable, but I should have known to approach the situation that had been created with great caution. I used an image of her to poke fun of her on Instagram not realizing at the time how many lines I was, in fact, crossing. The image I used and the comments I wrote blasted her and were clearly embarrassing. First off, I had no right to use the photo I used of her as it did not belong to me. I located the image from her own personal photos. Secondly, I grossly misread the fragility of our situation. She blocked me on Instagram with good reason. I didn't stop there. I continued to make light of unique circumstances. I went on Facebook and came up with, what I believed, to be a clever way of telling her how I still felt about her. She blocked me on Facebook. I could care less. I was flying way too high to pick up on the clear message. If nothing else, she needed time away from my ongoing games.

My family knew there was a problem, but didn't know the right course of action. They took control of my financial responsibilities. By Christmas they knew they had to get me into a psych ward; I needed serious help. I was hearing only what I wanted to hear. I was urging myself further and further into psychosis. I was drawing conclusions about who people close to me were in their past life. I thought I was King Tut reincarnated. I spent day after day laying in my bed laughing hysterically. I lost all sense of responsibility. I deserved what came next because it was the only way to bring me back to the real world.

On New Year's Eve of 2018, my brother and sister entered my apartment and coerced me to grab a bite to eat. My mind was all over the place. My emotions were in and out of hysteria and anger. I have no way of explaining this particular behavior. I had brought myself there in my time of self-isolation. We went out to eat at a Vietnamese restaurant in my neighborhood. I couldn't sit through the meal and make conversation. I was acting instinctively, but quite clearly irrationally. My brother and sister had full intention of bringing me to a hospital. They were just doing so cautiously as they knew I would lose total control if they didn't proceed in the interaction in a delicate manner. They knew full well that if I sniffed out their plan to get me a psychiatric evaluation I would absolutely refuse. The meal ended and we got back into the car. My brother asked me if I thought it was best if we make our way to the hospital. I agreed, thinking that we would be going to have my sister checked out.

Well, I might know better than anyone how to get myself out of being admitted to the psych ward and given a psychiatric evaluation, but there was no fooling anyone this time around. It took a little trickery, but they got me on a hospital bed in front of a doctor. The doctor couldn't even control the conversation as I unraveled immediately. Despite all kinds of feelings I was experiencing heading into the hospital, despite my disdain for psych wards, despite my uncontrollable erratic behavior, when I got in front of the doctor I was beyond jovial. I was happy and giggly. I opened up about the false reality I was creating in my mind without any restraint; without thinking about how my answers were sure to get me admitted to the hospital's psychiatric unit for the fifth time in my life. Honestly, the whole evaluation became quite enjoyable. Even the doctor had to hold back her laughter. The fantastical world I was finally letting someone gain access to wasn't bad or evil in any way. The world I created was happy, and so was I.

It's a misconception that people with bipolar disorder and undergoing manic episodes are thinking horrible thoughts. Quite the opposite. Mania on many accounts is beautiful and blissful for the person in that state. Many times, I have found myself crying uncontrollably thinking about how unremarkably wonderful life truly is. I spent time hanging around my brother's place of work. One of his employees would observe my behavior and tell me, "Will, you're crazy." I would look at her and tell her the truth, "Yeah, but I'm the good kind of crazy." I hate when some psychopath shoots up a school or goes on a deadly rampage, and sure enough, it hits the news that the person happens to be bipolar, as if that's some type of excuse. I don't buy it one bit. That's just not what's going on in my head. When I'm manic or hypomanic, I think good thoughts. I think about the goodness in mankind and humanity as a whole. In my psych evaluation that attitude and those thoughts prevailed. It didn't mean that I was free to go, but it meant that mania isn't something to fear. It's okay to be relentlessly happy and have unimaginably happy thoughts; you just have to be brought back to the real world so you can function in society accordingly.

They wheeled me up to the hospital's psych unit. I changed clothes and went to bed. The realization that I was back in the mental institution had not yet kicked in. I woke up the next day, and quickly became aware of my surroundings of which I had become all to familiar with in the past couple of years. An immediate switch got flipped in my head. Not only did I go into hospitalization mode, but I started the process of figuring out just exactly where my mind had led me and where my train of thought had gone astray.

Chapter 27
Prepared to Rehab from Psych Ward Experience

I was more lost than I had ever been in my life. Even my first mental collapse had some strain of logic that went along with what ultimately led to my original psychosis. This time, however, I had brought myself to the precipice. Everything I was thinking that was mental was created in my own mind. Luckily, I had been through this before. I knew I needed to be checked. I also knew exactly what the hospital would do to test me. I was prepared to work on my rehabilitation right away.

I was officially a patient admitted to the psych unit in Swedish Covenant hospital. The doctors and staff had no idea the patient (me) that they would spend the next fifteen days dealing with. I might have been completely mental, but I wasn't looking to social workers and nurses for answers. I didn't need to be broken down to know right away that I had lost it. I accepted that fact on my own. I just needed to figure out just how out of touch and off-base I really was. That would take time, but I was confident that it was something I could figure out on my own. Using the phones to call members in my family, I picked up on clues to help piece myself back together. I didn't exhibit any problems as far as the eye could see. I confided in no one. What had been going through my head before being admitted needed to be forgotten. I had to start fresh. I walked the hallway as I tend to do and began the recovery process internally and on my own.

I don't kid around about the mindset I have regarding psych wards. There's only one way out of these types of places, and that's to escape. In reality, the only way to escape is to take the necessary steps to gain the social workers' and nurses' (who, by the way, record everything you do, say, and even eat) favor. They then must alert your assigned doctor that you, the patient, are well enough to leave. The doctor then goes about signing your release and you stroll right out, mentally sound and stable, or not. That's always the right play, the only play, and should be considered plan A. I was scoping out plan B and C because I wasn't getting straight answers from my doctor from the very beginning. Plan B: Scope out the escape routes, find a weakness, and wait for the right moment to bolt. The elevator was out of the question. There were three main doorways along the hallway. I wanted to see how well-guarded they were. I made enough of a scene to find out that the staff had a plan of action to lock and stand guard at each exit if they sensed a possible problem. Plan B was out of the question. Plan C could've worked. I used hospital socks, towels, and the rubber-like casing on the bed pillows to create makeshift shoes. I used a pillowcase, stuffed it with towels, and ripped another towel apart to create a formidable backpack. The idea was simple. Break a window in the common area with a chair. Jump out the window. It was a two-story fall. There was a bush at ground level. Land on my back with the backpack stuffed with towels to help break my fall. Roll off the bush and make a run for it. The staff confiscated my shoes and backpack before I had a chance to try out Plan C. I doubt I would've ever gone through with it, but I was willing to, at least, think of anything to get out of these types of places.

My stay at Swedish Covenant psych ward turned out to be one of the scariest moments in my life; probably the scariest. In seven days, I was ready to be released. I had worked through all my shit. I needed those first seven days to get under control and work my mind back to stability. I met with my doctor. He said that he couldn't let me out until my parents came to the hospital to pick me up. I called my parents. They said they weren't going to be able to come get me until the doctor told them that it was okay for me to be picked up. It was a catch-22. I spent eight more days in the psych ward searching for answers. There were none. The doctor's story stayed the same and so did my parents. There was no truth. It was sickening. I was left trapped and completely hopeless. I was being lied to by my doctor and my parents. Worse, I had no clue if I was ever getting out of that place. I had taken all the necessary steps required of mental patients to show that I was ready to re-enter society. I lived in complete fear. It was straight out of a horror movie.

Finally, my brother and sister showed up in the psych unit to retrieve me. They had my doctor's permission. In my fifteen-day stay I had been injected with what us patients call bootie juice over nine times. (Bootie juice is a shot of anxiety medication administered to patients that act out of line or become unruly. The shot itself hurts a little, but for a guy of my size does very little, and in my opinion is an archaic form of punishment.) I had been strapped down in five-point restraints on three different occasions; I had been tackled in the hallway by three security guards because I refused to go to my room after a staff member's arbitrary request; I had used the hospital phones to call 911 and reported that I was being held captive. I couldn't wait to leave. I was never looking back.

My life after the last psych ward visit was handled by my family inappropriately. I went from being monitored by nurses and social workers to being monitored by my own sister. My parents were on a vacation in the Galapagos Islands and left my sister in charge of my day-to-day. They had taken my car and hid it from me. They had taken my driver's license, my social security card, and birth certificate. They assumed full control.

Chapter 28
I Still Wasn't Free

I went along with the game my family was playing the best I could. It was madness. My brother, my biggest supporter and ally, wanted nothing to do with what was going on. He removed himself from the absurdity with just cause. He admittedly was torn between the opposing sides. He saw reason for the treatment I was getting but had to take a back seat as he knew it was a recipe for disaster. I had a supply of medication to take, but I also needed to touch base with my psychiatrist now that I was out of the hospital. I had only met with this specific psychiatrist one time before … a meeting my mom happened to have come to. Nevertheless, I had an appointment to see her in the immediate future. My mom told my sister that the psychiatrist meeting, which I lined up while in Swedish Covenant, no longer existed. She made up the notion that the particular psychiatrist in question wouldn't take my insurance. Upon her return from vacation, my parents would go about helping me find a suitable out-patient psychiatrist. In other words, they were going to pick a doctor of their liking. It was all bullshit. The idea that the psychiatrist wouldn't take my insurance was a lie made because my mom didn't like that particular doctor. Again, my parents were assuming full control of every detail of my life, and it only got worse.

I was not only unamused by the charade, pissed off as well, but starting to fear what my life was turning into. I knew every play that was being made before it ever happened. My parents returned from vacation and it took less than 24 hours before I completely lost my cool. I erupted. It was an immediate fight, and I was fighting for the right to have independence. My livelihood was at stake. One argument led to the next. Pretty soon my mom's plan unraveled. After all, the move had already been made years before. She wanted to keep me at her house and under her watch. As if we hadn't been through this before. My parents found it completely acceptable to play doctor and hospital with my life. Now I know, it didn't help that I had no job. It didn't help that they were paying my bills. It also didn't help that they were taking away my freedoms. How could I get a job without my ID or social security card? How could I get myself together and on my own feet if they went about chopping off my legs? You can argue all you want that they had the right to do what they were doing, but I don't buy the argument that this was ultimately going to help me.

My mom had me alone in her car and ready to take me back to her apartment for bed. It was a fight. I told my mom that I wanted to hang out with my brother who lived close by. I lied that he was expecting me. She agreed to drop me off at his apartment under the condition that I walk back to her place after I was done hanging out. I had a phone, but no wallet. My parents had the keys to my own apartment. I saw no other option. I marched to Northwestern emergency room for a psych evaluation only one week removed from earning my release from my last psych ward visit.

Chapter 29
My Last Psychiatric Evaluation

The hospital took my request seriously and I was brought to a room with three other men. My read of the three men was that they were all homeless looking for a warm bed during the cold Chicago winter. They were all asleep. I grabbed a chair and acted accordingly. I did my best to fit in with the other three guys. I took off some of my clothes and did my best to fall asleep. When in Rome. More and more people cycled in and out of the observation room I was clearly in. Some were drunk people others were clearly dealing with psychiatric issues of their own. It took hours, but I finally fell asleep. They promptly woke me up and started questioning me; they were probing into my story trying to get honest answers in order to evaluate whether or not my story held water and to assess my mental state fairly. I passed the observation room test and got taken to another floor for further observation and questioning.

My story was obscure and unique. Again, I found myself on the run from my parents' control. I showed up to the emergency room with the request to get a psychiatric evaluation. I was completely stable. I had zero intention of being admitted to another psychiatric facility. I wanted to be administered an evaluation in order to be cleared that night. I knew if I showed up at my parents' apartment there would be a fight. I assumed that they would try to take me to an emergency room themselves. I was predicting their next move. I figured if I went about getting a clear evaluation on my own, and hours later they brought me into an emergency room for an evaluation, they would end up looking insane. It was a far-fetched belief, but I was in a pretty far-fetched predicament.

I was in a familiar position. On a hospital bed in a hospital being monitored for any type of unusual behavior. I accepted the notion that I could be headed back to the psych ward. Before any further questions had been asked or answered I started the pro-cess any mental patient needs to go through once admitted to a psych ward. I was staying steps ahead. I set up a doctor's meeting in two weeks -- a requirement for psych patients to do before be-ing released from the psych ward. I had no credit card and I ended up calling my aunt for her credit card number so I could pay for the visit in advance. I began the process of finding work as well. Of course, this was more for show than anything else.

Hours upon hours went by. They were waiting for me to fall asleep. It felt like over 12 hours passed, but truthfully, I have no idea. Finally, I fell asleep. They woke me up and brought me in for questioning. They wanted to see if I held firm to my original story. I was beyond exhausted and could barely put together full sentences. I was brought into a room with five doctors. I read the room vibe immediately. Three doctors sat to my left. They were younger, my age. They weren't there to ask the questions or pass any judgment. They were observing. They were there to learn and gain insight into how to handle a situation such as mine. In front of me was the head honcho. He had a computer in front of him … taking notes. Behind him was the doctor taking a back seat in the process. He was in clear opposition with the doctor adminis-tering the ongoing conversation. He was on my side. If I kept my cool, it would be that doctor that had the ability to veto any future hospitalization.

I couldn't stop talking. I didn't even need to be prompted with questions. My story and situation were spilling out. I was scared. I didn't want to go back to any psych ward for any amount of time. I was fresh out of a fifteen-day stay one week prior. I was in hysterics, but I was doing okay. Then I slipped up. I knew I was slipping up, but I couldn't help myself. My story was hard enough to explain on a full night's sleep. Trying to get my point across and explain my story completely sleep-deprived proved impossible. I was in tears begging helplessly for mercy. I knew the head doctor had made up his mind before I ever entered the room. My story was just too fantastical to be real or sane. I told the five doctors that nobody believes the guy who's already labeled crazy. Nobody believes crazy.

As soon as I contradicted myself, I got the signal that my interrogation was over, and I had lost. The doctor taking the back seat in the process dropped his head clueing me into the fact that he could no longer have my back. I tried to bring my story back together briefly. I couldn't save myself. I had lost the room and I knew it. I stopped caring. I flipped out on the main doctor who had made up his mind long before. I stormed out of the room angry and defeated. I had to prepare myself for another psych ward visit.

Time marched on in the emergency room. They were waiting for me to fall back asleep before transporting me to my next destination. They didn't want to wheel me off while I was awake because I could become unruly. I stayed wide awake. Finally, they gave up and called in the ambulance team to ship me away. I was being brought to a familiar location. Methodist hospital on the north side of Chicago. My first time in Methodist was no picnic. This next time would prove to be considerably harder.

I went through the onboarding procedure and was sectioned to Section 5C. I signed into the hospital and immediately requested to sign my five-day. I had no plans to stay long and wasted no time exercising my right to be evaluated over the course of the next five days and granted my release. Of course, if a patient is not granted their release in five days, then they have the right to a court hearing to state their case. It was late at night. I got pointed in the direction of my room and went to bed. The next day proved to be the first of what became quite an eye-opening experience.

Chapter 30
The Fight Nobody Should Ever Have to Face

I woke up. I had slept through breakfast catching up on rest I badly needed. I stepped out of my room to start walking the hallway as I tend to do. Immediately, I found myself taking in my current surroundings and assessing my new living quarters. In my previous five institutionalization experiences, the living arrangements were coed. Sure, men and women often times had different sections of the facility that the opposite sex was not allowed to enter, but Methodist 5C was all men. Specifically, all black men. There were approximately 30ish patients in this facility ranging from ages 18-65. I was the only white guy. In the first three steps out of my room on the first day, the tone was really clear. I was not only the fresh meat in the place, but I was automatically the enemy. I was the enemy because I was white. I had a target on my back the size of the state of Illinois. A lot of these guys had a problem with the system or circumstances they had been given in life, and I was a representation of that problem based on skin color alone. I didn't falter. I treaded carefully, but I walked the hallway with my head held high.

Lunch came around, and I would be lying to you if I wasn't looking forward to it. I was near the end of the line to state my name and receive my tray of food. The stage was set. The majority of the group filled the three tables on the right. A few guys sat at one of the two tables on the left. One of the tables on the left was completely vacant. I was handed my tray of food and didn't miss a beat. I took an open seat at the middle table on the right with most of the other guys. I wasn't looking for any type of approval. I remained completely unflustered. I took a look at my food, found my fork, and acted as if I had been there before; for all intents and purposes, I had. Before I could get my first bite of food to my mouth the sound off began. "Black Panther Party fifth generation." "Black Panther Party third generation." "Black Panther Party first generation." I didn't flinch and didn't acknowledge the attacks. I ate everything on my tray, got up from the table, and went back to walking the hallway. All eyes were on me. The group was trying to get under my skin. They wanted a reaction. I gave them jack shit.

I wasn't in this place to make friends. I was there to serve my five days and get out. I didn't ask questions, and nobody asked me any questions. I barely spoke a word, especially in the first couple of days. My personal circumstance was bigger than the racial discrimination going on around me. I didn't make a single phone call, but my parents had tracked me down. They contacted my doctor and established a dialogue that brought me favor.

Many years ago, back when I was still enrolled in college, my parents convinced me to create or at least sign a completely legal document giving away my power of attorney to my parents. The idea behind the document was to allow my parents to take control of my well-being if I was ever legally and medically considered insane. The document was made to protect me from any future hospitalization I might face moving forward. It made sense at the time. My understanding was that my parents could use this power of attorney document to spring me from any psych ward no questions asked. My parents were officially activating this power of attorney document in order to take me out of the psych ward I was currently in.

The catch in all of this was simple yet crazy. I was on the run from my parents' control. I didn't want to be let go in their custody. I wanted nothing to do with them. The doctor I had in 5C was the same doctor I had years earlier when I was admitted to Methodist 5 South. He knew I hadn't reached out to my parents. They tracked me down on their own. I waived the right to have visitors. I made no phone calls. I made it clear to the doctor that I wanted to be evaluated over the next five days and walk out of the hospital of my own fruition. He supported me completely. My parents threw their legal power of attorney in my doctor's face, and he spat all over it.

I was assigned a social worker to my case that worked along-side my doctor. The social worker, by my judgment, was a lawyer making an appearance at the hospital to help with my case and my case alone. She was only around for the first three days. The three of us went through the power of attorney document. She point-ed out to the doctor that the way this thing was worded might actually give my parents some merit if it did in fact go to court. The doctor looked at the social worker and said, "Watch this." He turned to me and said, "Will, if we were in court and you were asked who holds your power of attorney, what would you say?" I announced adamantly, "Me." The doctor turned back to the social worker and said, "See, that's all any judge will ever have to hear." The social worker didn't offer a rebuttal. She had been thoroughly convinced. She turned to me and said she was leaving at the end of the day and would no longer be my social worker. In other words, her job here was done.

The patients in 5C overheard a lot of my conversations with my doctor and social worker. One of the guys asked if I was some sort of child star. They were quickly becoming aware of my prob-lems. They were warming up to my story and respected the fact that I was going through some seriously messed up shit. The guys in the psych ward went from an attitude that I represented the white man and white authority. They rallied around the Black Pan-ther insignia. Pretty soon I was being called "The White Panther." I loved it.

My doctor set up a phone call between my parents and myself with him acting as the intermediary right before I was all set to leave. He wanted to establish ground rules to protect me when I got out. My mom and dad were on the line as my doctor and I sat together with his phone on speaker. The disgusting truth became apparent. My dad let out his intention. He was to have full control over most aspects of my life. It didn't stop there. He intended to be in full control of my medication, not just administering the medication, but deciding what medication I was to take. He was to choose my psychiatrist and work directly with the psychiatrist to determine the appropriate course of action to somehow control my bipolar. My doctor from Methodist Hospital listened to both my dad and mom. He couldn't believe what he was hearing. He quite literally explained to my parents that what they wanted to do, what they believed was the right thing to do and the necessary course of action, was quite literally crazy. He used those words. He called my dad crazy about three or four times. That doctor helped me take my life back. He knocked my parents off their ridiculous pedestal and won me the fight and my freedom. I wasted no time once I got out of the psych ward; I wrote my own power of attorney and got it notarized … I think I made close to ten copies.

Well, it didn't take long after my trip to 5C to get my life back. My parents backed down and respected my space and my process. I wasn't home free. I still had a lot of growing up to do. I still had to take responsibility over my own life. I had been given more than every advantage one could ask for to be able to do such a thing. I still was living too carefree. I was still taking advantage of my parents' credit card. The difference at this time was that I was using it to purposely piss them off. I was using it at an absurd rate to get even with them.

I was fresh out of Methodist 5C and I made another mistake reaching out to the girl who was quite clearly trying to erase me from existence. I had been locked out of my normal Twitter account. I have no way of explaining why or how. I made a new Twitter account with no intentions whatsoever. I mentioned long ago that nobody loses their mind and casually snaps back to normal. It takes time. I had snapped back from the insanity I faced in December 2018 as quickly as one could. I wasn't fully there despite having a clear mind; despite making it through two trips to two different psych wards. I was grasping at straws trying to find answers to questions that I had no business asking. I was more alone than ever. The mountain I had to climb to get back in the real world was staring me down in the face, and I wasn't ready to start the climb. Was I in any way shape or form insane doing what I did on my new Twitter account? Hell no! I just wasn't accepting the reality. I thought that maybe the girl might be clued into what

I had just been through in the past month or so. Completely false. I tweeted to her if she would be willing to be my power of attorney. I was just making light of my own situation. I was poking fun at the very notion of allowing somebody else to have or hold my power of attorney. I meant no harm, but, in retrospect, I see how this tweet could be quite alarming and ridiculously creepy. It was out there for everyone to see. Poor form, I know. I was subsequently blocked on Twitter, rightfully so. That was it. I was all out of any other options. I was left picking up my life and trying my best to sort through the mess of my shattered heart.

Chapter 31
Too Much to Fight For

By the beginning of March 2019, I finally accepted my long over-due wake-up call. I signed up for Uber and started the process of making my own money and paying my own bills. Everything I had to pay for was put back in my name. The process wasn't that simple. I was still battling my parents for autonomy over everything. I started a bank account that they were unaware of. I found a new doctor that had no contact with them and would not be permitted to reach out to them under any circumstance. All this shit I went through made me more headstrong than ever. I was always thinking about the next step I had to take. For the first time in my life, I was planning and preparing for the future. This was never my M.O. I tend to live in the moment and take action as it comes my way. It took 32 ½ years, but I was finally acting like a grown-up with the resolve to be able to always be able to take care of myself.

By April 2019, I picked up a full-time server job at an amusement bar. About a month into my new job, my car had officially broken down. It could still drive, but a major part that connected to the engine was shot. It was all for the best. Just before I hit 200,000 miles in less than four and a half years, I drove my car into my garage and put it in park for the last time. I wasn't home free. I was making just enough to pay all my bills, other than my phone bill, but just barely. As the summer season moved forward, it became clear that I was going to make it. I was even starting to save money, and the restaurant job was only picking up.

The mounting hospital bills I faced offered a whole nother challenge. In the past three years, I had been admitted to four different psych wards. I had been asked to undergo six emergency room psychiatric evaluations. The costs proved to be outrageous. Quite simply, impossible to even begin to pay. Add all the bills up and I was over $15,000 in debt. Here I was, going to hospitals with manic depression. Generally, after a manic episode, depression tends to follow with many people with bipolar disorder. I was treated for mania. What better way to send a person into depression than sticking them with a $5,000 hospital bill? I applied for financial assistance to a few of the hospitals. Swedish Covenant was the only hospital to even respond to my requests. My bill dropped from thousands of dollars to $300. I paid them in full. To this day, not a single other hospital has received a dime from me. They all went about selling off my hospital fees to debt collectors. I welcome all the calls these parasitical institutions send my way. I have no intention of ever paying them a penny. If they take me to court and win their case, then they legally will be able to collect on my debt. Until that day comes, I am not prepared to make any payment at the time, and I am unable to go about setting up a payment plan to pay off that debt. One debt collector asked me if I had family or friends that I could ask for money to help pay off the debt. I lost it, "What, you want me to shake down my friends and family … you want me to go out on the street with a McDonald's cup begging for pennies on the corner, and then you want me to give you those pennies …," I continued on for five minutes giving this guy a piece of my mind. That debt is mine and mine alone. The burden to pay that debt lies on me and me alone. How dare you think it is okay to ask me to place the burden of that debt on other people.

The girl has never left my thoughts. I stopped trying to send her messages through social media platforms. I found myself texting her every so often. Figured what I always figured; if she didn't want to get my texts, she had every right in the world to block me on her phone. I was up late in bed unable to fall asleep one night. I was thinking about her. I texted her for the first time in quite a while. I have no clue if she even got the text. I said what was on my mind. Within twenty minutes, I fell asleep. I mean no harm and hope I'm not harassing her. If texting this girl helps me fall asleep and sleep is the most important factor in my mental stability, then I'm left with no other option. I love her. I know I have to move on, but I don't know how long that will take or if it will ever happen. I think it's funny, given everything I've been through and everything I know, that I'm being blocked on every platform. I even made sure to get blocked on Venmo. I wanted to. I'm trying to turn it into a joke. Perhaps making fun of the whole blocking thing is not a joke to her at all. Finding humor in it all is the only way I know how to cope with her vanquishing from my life. I wish it wasn't that sad and pathetic. I wish it wasn't creepy. I wish our story wasn't for nothing. I wish there was a better result -- one that wasn't so tragic. I prefer crazy (really crazy) love story over tragedy every day of the week.

This is the part where those two final words appear. I can't write: The End. I refuse. Instead, I offer a conclusion in hopes there is still hope. People with bipolar disorder go through some intense and unexplainable highs and lows. They should be encouraged to share how they came to feel and reach those emotions. Our stories are incredible. We tend to see it all, admittedly aspects of reality that aren't even there to be seen. Our perspectives are unique. We have a heightened sense of awareness of our surroundings and tend to get every situation we are part of because we spend countless hours analyzing and overanalyzing every encounter that develops in front of us. They say that you shouldn't judge a person until you walk a mile in their shoes. Try on some of our shoes. The perspective on life you might gain will not only surprise you but may even change how you view all things moving forward. Be careful, however, we have our own insecurities and our own set of fragilities. We spent a long time being cast out, and even longer working our way back. It can be hard to open up and explain ourselves because many times we are unable. Excuse the errors of our ways; we tend to attack situations in ways that can be so peculiar it may not make sense. Stick with us. The logic is there, it's just in an abstract form. There is a method to the madness, I promise.

For Now

ABOUT THE AUTHOR

Will Morro is a graduate of Boston College with a B.A. in Sociology, where he played Division 1A Club Rugby. He was diagnosed with Bipolar Disorder I at the age of 20. Enduring six hospitalizations in mental health facilities and nine psychiatric evaluations in emergency rooms over the past 13 years, he confronts his illness, his life, his family and his friends head-on in this debut memoir. He lives in Chicago and plays golf at every opportunit

www.ingramcontent.com/pod-product-compliance
Lightning Source LLC
Chambersburg PA
CBHW070718250726
48662CB00001B/469